The Road to Athletic Scholarship

The Road to Athletic Scholarship

What Every Student-Athlete, Parent, and Coach Needs to Know

Kim McQuilken

New York University Press • New York and London

NEW YORK UNIVERSITY PRESS
New York and London

Library of Congress Cataloging–in–Publication Data

McQuilken, Kim, 1951–
The road to athletic scholarship: what every student-athlete,
parent, and coach needs to know / Kim McQuilken.
p.   cm.
ISBN 0-8147-5530-5 (cloth: alk. paper). — ISBN 0-8147-5546-1
(pbk. : alk. paper)
1. College sports—Scholarships, fellowships, etc.—United States.
I. Title.
GV351.M38   1996
796'.071'173—dc20   96–19530
                    CIP

New York University Press books are printed on acid-free paper,
and their binding materials are chosen for strength and durability.

Manufactured in the United States of America

10 9 8 7 6 5 4 3 2 1

DEDICATED to Scott and Brett,
both of whom have created for me
my most exciting moments in sports.

Contents

Preface   ix

1. The Essence of Sports and the   1
   Student-Athlete

2. The Parents' Role   9

3. Athletic Scholarship: Who Makes
   the Rules?   27

4. Athletic Scholarship: What's Available?   31

5. Eligibility for Scholarship   43

6. The Recruiting Process   53

7. Recruiting Misconceptions   71

8.   The Marketing of a Student-Athlete   75

9.   The Final Decision   83

10.   The Walk-On   87

11.   The High School's Role: How To Build Your Plan   95

12.   Important Questions   105

13.   Step-by-Step Guide   115

14.   Appendix   121

   Index   169

Preface

This guide has been designed to assist parents, student-athletes, and high school administrators and coaches through the college selection and recruitment process. Gifted young men and women interested in pursuing their athletic and academic dreams need help in the decision-making process of college selection. Parents and student-athletes are all too often passive bystanders in the recruiting process rather than aggressive participants preparing for the student-athlete's future. Most parents and students believe they are captives of a process that may or may not come knocking at their door.

Families can, and should, take a more active role in designing the student-athlete's future. At the very least, this role can broaden the range of academic and athletic options available to the candidate. At best, family participation can greatly increase the student-athlete's chances of an academic or athletic scholarship at the college or university level.

Furthermore, high school athletic programs should be active contributors to assisting deserving student-athletes in reaching the next level. High school administrators and coaches need to understand the complexities of the college recruiting process. They must also develop a response for recruiters that will enhance the chances of athletic scholarships for their student-athletes.

This book will familiarize you with NCAA(National Collegiate Athletic Association) recruiting rules and ways of using them to your advantage. It will educate you about the types of athletic scholarships available and how they may be combined with other forms of financial assistance, and it will introduce you to the college coach's perspective of the recruitment process, thereby fully defining what it means to be "recruited." Most important, this book places the process, actual school selection, and college athletic experience in the proper perspective.

1. The Essence of Sports and the Student-Athlete

My road to athletic scholarship, and later, to seven years in the National Football League (NFL), should be an inspiration to all underdogs and overachievers in sports. As a starting quarterback at William Allen High, a public school in Allentown, Pennsylvania, with three thousand students in grades ten through twelve, I was fairly tall (six foot, one inch), very skinny (149 pounds), and slow (4.9 seconds in the forty-yard dash)—most definitely not a candidate for the *Parade* All-America Team. In fact, I didn't make the All-State Team, and, if the truth must be known, I was not even named to the East Penn All-League Team. So you see, recruiters were not exactly falling over themselves to lure me to their schools.

From these humble athletic origins I emerged in the 1974 NFL draft as the Atlanta Falcons' second selection. Critical decisions made at crucial phases in my development marked my path to the NFL. In retrospect, I cannot take much credit for these decisions. They were a combination of positive parental influence, instinct, circumstances, and, yes, some good luck. These were accompanied by hard work, discipline, excellent coaching, and a college program at a Division 1-AA institution that provided the optimal environment for someone like me—no superstar but a determined student-athlete.

My father was a constant force in this process, driving me to fulfill my potential. At the same time, he had the uncanny ability never to pressure me to complete a level of achievement that he had predetermined. As a high school sophomore I was strictly junior varsity material, and my father simply wanted me to be the best on that team; there was never any mention of my moving up to the varsity level. He was similarly supportive throughout my entire career. I know now that he was a very rare individual and the key element in the early development of my confidence. Despite his restraint, however, I never doubted his enthusiasm. Even in front of eighty thousand screaming fans, I had to listen only for a minute to know where he was sitting!

When it came time to choose a college, peer pressure was undoubtedly a factor. My best friends were going on to Princeton, Virginia, and William and Mary, all high-profile academic schools. I was torn between trying to walk on (that is, try out for the team without being recruited) at a big school or opting for another year of development at a prep school that would offer a partial scholarship. My father made it clear he would be happy wherever I chose to play, as long as I maximized the opportunity. In my heart I didn't believe I was ready for Division I football—and I was right. A year of prep school would, no doubt, add much needed inches to my wiry 150-pound frame. My instincts about the limits of my potential were very strong. I was certain I would end up fourth or fifth on some Division I depth chart early in my collegiate career if I attended a major football university.

Circumstances sometimes are the remedy to a dilemma. Ironically, after an excellent prep school season (and academic semester), I had grown only to a strapping 152 pounds. I had received exactly one scholarship offer, from an excellent academic institution with no football program to speak of—Lehigh University. Lehigh had not had a winning football season in ten years. I liked the academic challenge at Lehigh, but I wasn't sure about the football part of the equation. Fortunately, Lehigh had a very persuasive coach in Fred Dunlap. Coach Dunlap convinced me that all his team needed was a pass-oriented quarterback to lead it to the promised land of Division II football. My parents and I were also pretty convinced that he and his assistant Walt King were not leaving our living room until I signed. Lehigh, however does not offer full NCAA scholarships; Lehigh offers athletic scholarships based on the financial need of the prospective recruit and his family. (Lehigh now competes in Division 1-AA football and still offers the same type of need-based grant, as I discuss later.)

My sophomore year at Lehigh we sported an 8–3 record. Our senior year we won the Lambert Cup, recognizing Lehigh's as the best Division II team in the East. We were one of only eight teams to be selected to the NCAA Division II national playoffs, and the only such institution with need-based scholarships.

Even though I went on to play over a nine-year period for the NFL's Atlanta Falcons and Washington Redskins and for the Washington Federals in the USFL (United States Football League), I still reflect fondly on those critical developmental years at Lehigh, which enabled me to make the transition to the NFL. As an NFL rookie I was soon reminded how unusual for a professional player my origins were. During my first team breakfast, a large fullback from a major Division I conference was relating his experiences in the Cotton Bowl and Orange Bowl. He finally turned to me and inquired about my college origins. "Lehigh," I replied. "Lee High," he repeated with astonishment. "You mean they drafted you right out of high school?"

My unconventional path was, I am convinced, the only possible road to professional sports for me. I was clearly a late bloomer. It was paramount to my development that I be allowed to compete at a level that would cultivate my skills rather than erode my confidence. With the help of my parents, coaches, and counselors I was able to excel gradually, both academically and athletically. My enjoyment and satisfaction in contributing to a successful program for four years reflected a very fulfilling overall experience. My selection by the National Football League was simply a gratifying validation that the *level* of athleticism is not the critical factor. Rather, the overriding factor in a student-athlete's growth is that this process take place in an environment ideally suited for the individual's integrated personal development.

One of the enduring benefits from a professional sports career is exposure to student-athletes and their parents. Over the years I have had the pleasure of speaking and working with many student-athlete groups. I am always impressed by how student-athletes continue to take on greater challenges in the face of increased academic and athletic workloads. Each generation is truly better equipped than the former to expand their horizons.

In stark contrast to my own gradual success, young athletes today often have wildly unrealistic visions of their future. The expectations of both student athletes and their parents are becoming more and more distorted, recognizing only the "biggest" and the "best."

The rising tide of commercialism in sports has fed this distortion. As the athletes and the games become more and more skilled, fans of all ages set standards according to what they see on television. The marriage of the electronic media to sports has widespread ramifications. Contracts between the major TV networks and the NCAA now range in the hundreds of millions of dollars for individual sports such as football and basketball. College programs thus can compete for these attractive awards and contracts only by increasing their development costs. These costs include recruiting budgets, coaches' salaries, and state-of-the-art athletic facilities. They can sustain these increased costs and keep the "blue chip" athlete only by winning and winning big. It is therefore not surprising that Division I college coaches in the high-revenue sports earn more money than the professors and, in many cases, the presidents of their institutions. (By the same token, these coaches' job security is only as strong as last year's won–lost record.)

The result is a system in which a great deal of pressure filters down onto the high school athlete and his or her family. The "blue chip" student-athlete is inundated by letters, phone calls, and visits by recruiters from these highly competitive institutions. The vast majority of these recruiters are honest, sincere, and hardworking professionals. But the process continues to be tested by some coaches and programs that are on the edge of succumbing to the intense pressure of this competitive arena.

Athletics has evolved to an important part of our student-athletes' lives from origins that certainly precede the turn of the twentieth century. Educators have long recognized organized sports not only as a means of "working up a sweat" but as an important building block in the development and maturation of youth.

Competitive sports can be every bit as important as math, English and the arts in the total development of a student. The student-athlete should not be denied the exploration of his or her potential in all of these areas. By the same token, the pursuit of athletic achievement should not supersede the development of the other elements necessary for a well-rounded education.

The essence of sports is the developmental impact our

participation has on our character and well-being. The field of competition often parallels the challenges of life. We are made to understand the sacrifice needed for achievement, with no guarantees for success or failure. We encounter unforeseen challenges from our environment, our competition and ourselves. While participation as a student-athlete does not ensure lifelong success, competitive sports can help you develop a resilient ability to cope with the challenges life has in store for you.

The father and coach of a famous baseball pitcher was once asked how happy he must be, given all his son's victories. The coach wisely replied, "I am just as happy for the losses he has been forced to experience."

This anecdote nicely embodies the essence of sports. Framed in the right way, sports can develop an inner resource the student-athlete will retain for decades after the cheering has subsided. While First-Team All-America might, for some, be the icing on the cake, I can tell you that the icing tends to melt a bit over the years. But the fundamental elements that are nurtured within the student-athlete will pave the way for broader achievements later in life.

Your ultimate goal should be to select a program that will best provide for the completion of your student-athlete mission. Only a select few will experience the highest levels of competition in sports. The vast majority must, along with their parents, recognize that the mission is not always to reach *beyond* our capacities but rather to make the most of our potential within a particular environment, be it the Big Eight conference or the Little Three.

2.   The Parents' Role

Regardless of whether a person wins or loses I have always believed that the experience of athletic competition prepares one for other challenges life has to offer. There is one challenge, however, that caught me completely by surprise. It is without a doubt the most difficult challenge I have faced in sports. It is the responsibility of parenting a student-athlete.

My two sons both had very rewarding high school basketball careers. For eight consecutive years I attended almost all of their varsity games. It did not take long for me to begin to experience vicariously the ecstasy and suffering of the individual games, even individual plays, in which my sons were involved.

I soon found myself instinctively analyzing my sons' next opponent and anticipating their team's game plan. The day before my sons' games I began to feel a distinct queasiness in my stomach—just like when I myself was suiting up. The night before the game I would often sleep poorly. The day of the game my concentration at work was gone, and by the time I drove to the game, I was energized and excited. Unfortunately, as a parent, one builds up all this adrenaline and then is required quietly to take a seat in the stands. Playing the game, win or lose, your son or daughter has the opportunity to burn it all up. You, however, go home bouncing off the walls.

Parents walk a very difficult line between supporting and encouraging their child to maximize his or her potential, on the one hand, and keeping their expectations on a realistic level. The challenge to parents intensifies as high school graduation draws closer. As the college years approach, parents realize that their child's success might offset, partially or completely the ever-rising costs of a college education. It therefore becomes difficult for any parent to evaluate objectively a son or daughter's potential to compete successfully at the collegiate level.

There are, statistically, very few "blue chip" athletes, who rise above the pack and are easily recognized as future college stars. The majority of scholarship athletes, though perhaps standouts when in high school, simply cannot compete successfully at the Division I college level.

The Young Superstar

The process really begins in the child's formative years. Children go through so many changes early in life that it is extremely difficult for any parent to form a lasting opinion about the athletic potential of his or her offspring. There are always children who jump out ahead of the pack early in life: the Little League baseball player who hits the daylights out of the ball or makes a habit of tossing no-hitters, the soccer player who runs rings around the opponents, or the swimmer whose times beat everyone by a wide margin.

These early achievements are all indications that potential exists. They are not, however, guarantees that the child's performance will continue to develop at the same speed throughout the maturation process. It is very important for the child to receive parental support and encouragement at this stage. But it is more important that the parent keep these early successes in perspective. I have witnessed dozens and dozens of recreational league superstars who were out of sports by the time they reached high school.

There are many reasons that an athlete might excel in the early years, only to be a nonparticipant at the high school level. Usually, it is nature that plays the biggest role. Some kids simply mature more quickly, physically or mentally. A bigger or faster body goes a long way in any league, but especially at the youth level. In contrast, a keen sense of what it takes to win will allow some kids to excel at a level beyond their peers. Either way, nature has a way of evening out the score for most kids. As natural evolution works on young athletes, it is important that parental support is properly dispensed. The worst reason that young athletes drop out is misplaced expectations and pressure applied by irrational parents.

Winning the MVP (most valuable player) award at age eleven or twelve is wonderful, but it also comes with a price. What does an eleven-year-old do for an encore? If the parent does not present the proper support mechanism, the child could face burnout by age thirteen or fourteen. Children mature unevenly within their peer groups. The awkward one today may be tomorrow's star.

It is important to acknowledge your child's successes. It is also important to remember that the other kids will probably close the gap in the next few years. When the child wakes up one day and is no longer the biggest or the fastest he or she will need the proper mental preparation to continue to succeed. If early successes have been blown out of proportion, the child may not have the resilience to compete on equal ground. The parent must work at teaching humility as well as at fostering success. The parent must practice humility with everyone associated with the child's athletic peer group, including teammates, opponents, coaches, and the child's own family. You must make a difference by example, and I guarantee your child will recognize it at any age.

Very few superstars have it all together at age nine, eleven, thirteen, or even sixteen. Remember that Michael Jordan did not make the basketball team during his sophomore year in high school! The evolution of a college scholarship player can be a slow, methodical process. Sometimes the prospect doesn't even resemble a candidate for future growth.

I mentioned earlier that I was a very late bloomer. Slow and skinny, I could easily have been discouraged at an early age. But I enjoyed a father who had a great knack for combining competitive juices with realistic expectations. I was always encouraged to excel, but I was never criticized for any lack of excellence.

Usually, a youngster with college potential will display some form of exceptional athletic ability. But the complete package will not necessarily manifest itself until later in life. As a parent, you may see a kid who has a great arm but lacks speed or ability. The smallest player on the team may have a tough-as-nails attitude. The shy nonleader may have excellent hand-eye coordination. Even if athletic potential is not reflected in batting average or sprint times or touchdowns, there is usually something that will catch your eye. The key for these late bloomers is to experience continual parental support and to practice, practice, practice.

Also remember that some athletes just are not ready for certain sports at early ages. Do not force a sport on a child, but go with the child's strength. The important factor is that the child begin to compete, even though the hand-eye coordination or the speed or the jumping ability may be a bit behind.

I have found that football, in particular, can be the wrong sport at an early age. Some youngsters just are not ready to hit or be hit, as required by youth football. I have also observed that parents of youth football players can become rabid in their enthusiasm for their child's success. An overenthusiastic parent may discourage a reluctant child from pursuing a game he or she might have excelled at later in life. You would be surprised how an athlete's mental toughness can change when the body matures. A great alternative sport for football in the early years is soccer, which is very competitive but lacks a lot of the banging of bodies required by football.

If a young athlete is going to continue to develop and mature, it will have to be according to his or her own schedule and not the parent's predetermined timetable. As parents, we walk a fine line between motivating our children to fulfill their potential and discouraging them with unrealistic expectations. Your student-athlete will be competing against his or her own expectations, his or her peer group, and sometimes even coaches. As a parent, do not provide another opponent for your student-athlete, but instead, be his or her biggest fan and supporter.

Parents and Coaches

One of the real challenges of parenting a student-athlete is identifying and cultivating your proper role in relation to the coach. No set formula for success exists in this area, but there are a great many ways to fail. As in any other profession, a wide range exists in sports in the quality of the coaches. The expertise and professionalism a coach displays is not necessarily directly related to a coach's placement at a particular level of competition. While you will generally find a high degree of expertise and commitment at the higher levels of competition, there are many exceptions, in both greater and lesser professionalism, at all levels. Therefore, the parents' degree of involvement is not tied to the student-athlete's level of achievement.

The majority of full-time coaches in junior high, high school, and college are competent and caring individuals. They are interested in helping young people succeed and put in a great deal of overtime to meet this challenge.

I have probably been spoiled by the high quality of the coaches I have played for throughout my career. My two junior high football coaches, Bill Roasch and Dick Trexler, were like gods to me. Excellent teachers and clean-cut role models, with even dispositions, they were my first impression of how an athlete should look, speak, and act.

My high school coach, Fritz Halfacre, stands as one of the greatest motivators I have ever played for at any level, including the NFL. He changed my life and the lives of many others before and after me. He tempered a disciplinarian approach with sensitivity to the individual. He instilled a work ethic that carried over to our personal lives and classroom work. If Coach Halfacre had a fault, it was being too sensitive and too caring. When he heard the voices of parental discontent, he listened, and at times he could be hurt by them. I learned in high school that even great leaders and motivators can be the target of petty, misguided, and self-interested abuse.

As a parent, your first and primary responsibility must be to let the coaches coach. Give the coach the opportunity to demonstrate his or her commitment before you commit to any type of confrontational role. Once you cross that line, you will live at odds with that coach throughout his or her tenure over your child. But the judgment between being a supportive parent on the sidelines and protecting the welfare of your child is the supreme challenge to us all.

I know of a family put right into the middle of this dilemma. Their son developed as an exceptional basketball player through elementary and junior high school. Brad was always the leading scorer and always named to the all-star teams. When he moved up to the high school level, it was no surprise that he made varsity as a sophomore and became a significant contributor throughout his sophomore season.

Most people felt Brad had college ball written all over him. He was a guard who would probably grow to six-foot one or six-foot two by his senior year. He was a good, if not a great, athlete who could shoot the trey as well an anyone in the county, and he was an excellent ball handler.

Prior to his junior year, Brad began to receive recruiting letters from colleges of all sizes. The game against his team's archrival in his sophomore year had been heavily scouted, and Brad had scored twenty-five points (including five three pointers). The word was out on Brad, and he was beginning to show up on college scouting reports.

Brad's father was a former athlete who took a great interest in his son's career and future. They always had a hoop set up in the driveway, and the two of them competed all the time. By Brad's junior year, his dad was convinced that he was college basketball material. To that end, they began to reply to the recruiting letters and hoped to have a good game film ready early in his junior year.

The head basketball coach at Brad's school was a hard man to read. He was clearly dedicated to the job and seemed to have a good fundamental understanding of the game. He did, however, have a temper and was known for his tirades at referees and his players during games. He was not one to hand out a lot of compliments, to his players or anyone else.

The real question for Brad's father was: Could he count on the coach for support with college recruiters? If you are a great player, it is possible to be recruited without the help of your high school coach. But only about 10 percent of all collegiate scholarship athletes were easily identified, "blue chip"–type players in high school. The remaining 90 percent had to be "discovered" by colleges, which usually takes a proactive coach, dedicated to advancing kids to the next level. Brad's father wasn't sure the coach was interested in his son's welfare, and he definitely wasn't sure what to do about it. For the time being, he elected to sit back and hope for the best.

Early in his junior year, Brad received a letter from the basketball coach at Notre Dame. Brad's high school coach also received a letter and a request for a film. Brad was leading his team in scoring, and the letters continued to come in. Brad's father casually addressed the issue of college with the coach, who cryptically responded he would answer requests. His reply did nothing to alleviate the father's concern about the coach's cooperation.

At the end of the year, Brad's father noted that while his son was receiving many introductory letters (from twenty-five to thirty) from college recruiters, there were few or no follow-up communications. This was hard to comprehend, since Brad had averaged fifteen points a game as a point guard and had provided excellent leadership on the floor. The father called Notre Dame to inquire about the status of the film and he was told the film had never been sent. Brad's father could not imagine a high school coach ignoring a request from one of the greatest academic and athletic institutions in the country. What was the problem?

At this point, the father felt he had no alternative but to meet with the coach and get some answers. He dreaded the meeting, knowing that if it went poorly, he would be risking any cooperation from the coach whatsoever. But timing was critical: recruiters had long lists of prospects, and slow responses might mean that Brad would be cycled to the end of the lists. Only a finite number of scholarships are available for the many deserving student-athletes. It was imperative that the high school coach respond in a timely manner and with a positive recommendation, or Brad might be left out in the cold.

Brad's father had an excellent relationship with the high school principal, who was an avid sports fan. He decided to ask the principal for advice on how to confront the coach. The principal also was concerned about the cooperation being provided by the coach. A check of the record revealed that the coach had not placed one of his players in a college program, big or small, in his three years as head basketball coach. The school was very large, with many athletes in other sports experiencing college success. Perhaps there was a problem here.

The principal suggested that the father and coach meet with him in his office after school. The premise of the meeting would not be to challenge the coach but for the father to make a general inquiry regarding the policy of both the school and the basketball program on the management of the recruiting process. Brad's father was motivated to keep it friendly. His own athletic experience told him that if he alienated this coach, then Brad's chances for a scholarship were nil. By the same token, if this coach was already sending out negative signals, either by his slow response or in direct testimony, Brad would again be the loser. Hence the meeting was necessary, and the format the father and principal selected was a reasonable course of action.

Unfortunately, it backfired. The coach came to the meeting with a chip on his shoulder. He said all the right things in front of the principal: of course he was interested in helping; yes he would proactively contact colleges, and he would do all he could. But he offered an observation that shocked Brad's father, reporting that while Brad was his best prospect, he wasn't sure Brad could play at the Division I level. Additionally, the coach had his own "professional" reputation with college coaches to consider, and therefore he must be very prudent when recommending any prospect to colleges. He admitted that he had dropped the ball on the Notre Dame film, but he would see to it immediately. He hoped that Brad could continue to

improve and rise to the level of a Division I recommendation.

Brad's father saw his son's dreams fading as he looked
in the eyes of the coach sitting before him. He now knew
this coach's bias would forever prevent him from supporting not only Brad but probably any athlete short of an NBA
first-round draft choice. It was later learned that this coach
had himself been a high school star who never played college ball. For his own reasons, he felt little compassion for
his players and little need to extend himself to help others
achieve what had eluded him. He had no intention of giv-
ing any of his athletes the benefit of his assistance. Brad's
father knew they were in trouble and would now have to
play catch-up with the colleges.

Brad and his father started by putting together their
own game film. The coach did make films available, and
they spliced together four halves of Brad's best performances from his junior year. Next, they created an information sheet on Brad (see chapter 8, "The Marketing of a
Student-Athlete") and sent it with tapes to twenty schools
that had initially contacted him. The problem with this tech-
nique was that it lacked the direct endorsement of Brad's
coach, who was more interested in a wait-and-see position
to "protect his reputation." Brad's dad wanted badly to
point out to the coach that his reputation was really one of
never having placed a player at the college level. He could
not understand why a coach wouldn't lend support to his
own player. Brad was a top scorer with decent size (now
six-foot one), a team leader who never missed practice, was

never in trouble at school. The college recruiter could decide if he was an inch or two too short or a step to slow. At any rate, the coach would never need to feel embarrassed for sticking his neck out for one of his own who was this qualified. Why not promote this type of player? Unfortunately, the answer in this case, and in many others that emerge every year around the country, is deeply rooted in the personalities of the high school coaches who mentor our student-athletes.

In Brad's case there was a bittersweet ending. After ruling out the option of transferring to another school (too late in career), Brad returned for his senior season and once again led the team in scoring, assists, and free-throw shooting. Although he received dozens of additional inquiries, he was not offered a scholarship. His father tracked down other college coaches who confirmed a lack of cooperation from the high school coach.

Brad's father wanted his son to try a junior college or a year of postgraduate prep school. Perhaps another year under a new coach would make a difference. Brad would have none of that—he was convinced he was college material. Brad's father strongly suggested a Division II or Division III school, but again Brad was not buying. Brad targeted a school in the Division I Southeastern Conference (SEC) and decided to enroll as a walk-on. (See chapter 10, "The Walk-On".) Even though the odds were greatly against him, he made the varsity team as a freshman walk-on. He dressed for all the home varsity games, played in several games, and scored his first collegiate points in the SEC. The coaching staff rewarded Brad for his contribution when they invited him to travel and dress for the season-ending SEC tournament. Brad's father could not have been prouder when he saw his son take the floor at the tournament. After the season, he couldn't have been angrier when the college coaches informed him that Brad's high school coach was crazy not to recommend Brad as a college prospect. They added that Brad and his father should not feel too bad because college coaches see this type of treatment more than they care to admit publicly.

As a parent, how would you have handled Brad's situation? It is difficult to criticize Brad's father for choosing the high road in the beginning. He chose to give his son's coach the benefit of the doubt. I still believe this is the best course of action. Once you have confronted a coach, there is usually no going back. I suppose Brad's father could have confronted the coach earlier and put him on notice that he expected a scholarship and would hold the coach accountable. Who knows? Perhaps fighting fire with fire does work sometimes. But in the final analysis, the chances for success remain highest if everyone involved is pulling in the same direction and not apart. As parents we must all try very, very hard to be supporters and not opponents of the student and the coach.

Parents and the Final Decision

As the student-athlete draws close to the selection of a college, many variables will contribute to a logical narrowing of his or her choices. These factors include:

- The student's academic level of achievement
- The curriculum preference of the student
- The student athlete's level of athletic achievement
- The response level and interest by college recruiters
- Student-athlete peer pressure
- Geographic considerations
- Financial constraints
- The Student-athlete's "feel" for the coaches and the institution
- Parental influence

The parental influence should be carefully weighted toward understanding the student's needs. Parents should avoid incorporating their own desires and needs (except financial needs) to the equation. Specifically, a student-athlete should strive for a level of athletic competition and academic achievement that best relates to his or her skills, not one targeted to respond to parental pressure and fulfill parents' expectations.

It is desirable for parents to keep the lines of communication open both ways; to and from your child. Continually discuss with your student-athlete the range of choices that exist in college athletics.

Even the "can't miss" high school star should be exposed not only to major colleges but also to medium-sized and small colleges. One tactical approach is to emphasize the academic and social highlights of lesser-known athletic

institutions. Another important step is to visit as many campuses as possible and provide the student-athlete with a
firsthand look at life on smaller campuses. Sometimes the
personal visit is the only way to recognize that smaller
schools can be attractive alternatives to the large universities athletes commonly see on television.

Getting out and visiting a cross section of campuses is a
good education for the parent as well as the student. It is
amazing sometimes how the warm, genuine smile of a
small-college coach will contrast with less-interested "big
time" coaches, who can afford to shop around. Parents need
to ask themselves, "Do I really want to turn over my child
to this environment?" After a personal visit, you will be in
a position to make an informed decision.

Parents must also get over the feeling, pervasive in this
country, that bigger is always better. I can't begin to tell
readers how often I have heard a parent boast about how
his or her student-athlete was going to the biggest school in
the region—when I knew their child should be considering
a program better suited to that person's skill level. Parents
need to advise and counsel but not force their child into situations.

One of the most difficult times for parents is the transition from actually directing our children to a position of *con-
sulting with* our children. While depending on the level of a
student's maturity, this transition often occurs during the
college selection process. (It is fair to say, however, that successful student-athletes may mature earlier in life, since they
have already accepted a role that inherently adds discipline,

sacrifice, and pressure to their lives.) Parents need to contribute a steady influence that broadens the perspective, but
they also need to recognize the student-athlete's ability to
make his or her own decisions.

3.   Athletic Scholarship: Who Makes the Rules?

The National Collegiate Athletic Association (NCAA)

As stated in the NCAA *Guide for the College-Bound Student-Athlete* (1995), the "NCAA is an association of member colleges that make certain rules governing eligibility, recruiting and financial aid." In other words, colleges and universities across the country that choose to be members of the NCAA agree to abide by the rules and regulations set forth by the membership.

Over one-thousand colleges and universities have been admitted to the NCAA since 1906. Currently, the NCAA consists of schools in the Division I, Division II, and Division III categories. Division I is subdivided into a Division 1-A and 1-AA category. Generally speaking, the divisions are a reflection of the degree of member schools' commitment to athletics. However, there are other criteria for placement in the various divisions, and a school may compete in one sport in one division and another in a different division, for instance, Division 1 in basketball and Division 1-AA in football. In all the divisions combined, the NCAA offers championship competition in over twenty-three sports, with the participation of over 250,000 athletes nationwide. (To learn more about the organization itself, write to the NCAA for the *Guide for the College Bound Student-Athlete* (1995) at the address listed in the Appendix).

The National Association of Intercollegiate Athletes (NAIA)

The National Association of Intercollegiate Athletes (NAIA) traces its origin to 1940. The NAIA has admitted into its membership nearly five hundred fully accredited four-year colleges and universities. Its focus is primarily on small to midsize schools, and it has pioneered the concept of a well-rounded athletic and academic environment for member institutions.

The NAIA provides a brochure, *A Guide for the College-Bound Student*, and the *NAIA Official Handbook*. You may obtain copies by phoning or writing to the organization at the NAIA headquarters (address and phone numbers are listed in the Appendix).

The National Junior College Athletic Association (NJCAA)

The National Junior College Athletic Association (NJCAA) was formed in 1938 to promote and supervise a national program of sports and activities for two-year colleges. The association consists of twenty-four regions nationwide and represents over five hundred junior colleges. The NJCAA provides competition for member institutions in twenty-four intercollegiate sports.

The association publishes an annual handbook that lists the school's geographical regions, calendar of events, substance-use and -abuse policy, eligibility requirements, and recruiting rules and regulations. NJCAA membership is classified by sports category into three divisions. Scholarships are available from NJCAA institutions competing in Division I and Division II. (For a complete listing of NJCAA requirements, write for the *NJCAA Official Handbook and Casebook* at the address and phone number found in the Appendix.)

Student-athletes may consider attending a junior college for a variety of reasons. Quite often, the junior college option is selected in a effort to improve grades or test scores for entrance into a four-year college. Prospects who were ineligible for admission or for scholarships to four-year schools directly out of high school may achieve eligibility status while attending junior colleges.

Standards for transfer from a junior college to a four-year college will vary from school to school. Generally, you are required to attend a junior college for two years; you then enter the four-year institution with two years of varsity eligibility remaining. However, there are exceptions to this rule and the requirements may vary depending on the four-year school's level of play (Division I, II, or III). Always receive confirmation from your targeted four-year institution regarding admission requirements, transfer procedures, and remaining eligibility *prior* to enrolling in junior college.

Another reason for the student-athlete to attend junior college may be to allow time to mature physically or emotionally. An extra year or two of physical growth can make a drastic difference during this formative period. Added pounds, increased strength and speed, and a more mature outlook on life are some of the important variables that recruiters look for in prospects. These attributes sometimes take longer to develop for some athletes, and junior college may be the best place to realize this growth.

Whatever your reason, the junior college option may provide the leverage needed to extend your student-athlete career. Even if the experience does not produce a college scholarship, the competitive spirit and championship format of the junior college environment can provide a lifetime of successful sports memories and lessons.

4.   Athletic Scholarship: What's Available?

The vast majority of parents and student-athletes are very concerned about their ability to fund a college education. Many believe that without the subsidy of a scholarship it is impossible to meet the rising costs of education. Consequently, it is important for everyone to know that other options do exist for funding a student-athlete's dream. The case of Matt Szczypinski is a wonderful example of successfully identifying and securing alternative financial resources for college.

Matt Szczypinski was a two-year football starter at Canevin High School in the greater Pittsburgh area. Since the age of seven, when he played Midget League football, his goal had been to become a college football player and ultimately a star at the Division I level of the NCAA.

Matt was always fairly big for his age; by the time he was a junior in high school, he stood at five feet, eleven inches, and weighed over two hundred pounds. As one of the bigger players on the team, he was a natural for the offensive guard and defensive tackle positions. But as Matt began to target colleges, he realized that while his size was appropriate for Canevin, he was woefully undersized for the Penn States and University of Pittsburghs of the Division I world.

Not to be denied, Matt approached his high school coach and inquired about moving to his old position of running back. He knew that his height and weight was more than adequate among Division I running backs. In good faith, his coach allowed him to work out at running back during spring training. However, it became apparent to Matt very quickly that the best place for him to help the team was on the line. That year Canevin was loaded with running backs but desperately needed linemen like Matt to spring the backs loose.

A team player, Matt moved back to his line positions for the start of the season and finished out his high school career as one of the top linemen in his conference. Due to his size, however, Matt was recruited only by Division III schools. These schools were very interested in Matt for both his athletic ability and his academic achievements.

Matt faced another serious hurdle, if he was going to play college football. NCAA Division III football programs do not offer athletic scholarships. Financial aid is offered only through the channels available to the general student body. While Matt's father made a nice living in the contracting business, financial aid was nonetheless a major consideration. Matt was one of seven children, including a brother already in college at the time and two sisters who would soon be considering college.

After carefully analyzing options during his senior year, Matt finally settled on Washington and Jefferson College. Washington and Jefferson is a private liberal arts school located in western Pennsylvania. Matt was impressed with the college's academic reputation, and he had developed an immediate rapport with the football coach, John Luckhart. Coach Luckhart had turned the Washington and Jefferson football program around to the point where the team was a perennial contender for the Division III national playoffs. In addition, the college had a fine liberal arts tradition, renowned for its high academic standards. The bad news was that a typical year of room, board, tuition, books, and expenses at the college cost approximately $20,000.

Matt and his family thus faced a big challenge. Fortunately, they had one big asset: Matt was a strong, consistent student throughout his high school career, graduating with a 3.2 grade point average (GPA). His scholastic efforts would literally pay off as his family began to explore its financial options.

They started with the general Washington and Jefferson College grant fund, which provided financial aid to students based strictly on financial need. The family filled out a detailed financial aid form (FAF) provided through the college financial aid office. A formula determines the family's eligibility for need, and the college decides on the amount of need that can be covered by the fund. Next, Matt turned to the Pennsylvania Higher Education Assistance Agency (PHEAA), which provides state-supported financial aid. Here again, Matt was successful in qualifying for aid that covered a portion of his costs.

While the college grant and the state assistance were significant, they did not cover the entire cost of a $20,000-per-year education. Undaunted, Matt discovered that Washington and Jefferson had an Entrepreneur Studies program that is funded by a trustee of the college. This program annually awards Eagle Scholarships to deserving students. Matt successfully applied for the Eagle Scholarship, which required essay responses on the application.

The Eagle Scholarship helped, but during the course of his college career Matt would require additional financial assistance. He turned to the federally funded Pell Grant and the federally subsidized Stafford loans to round out his financial aid package. But Matt's most inspirational idea for financial aid came from his mother.

One day, Matt's mother read in a trade advertisement at a local mall that families in the Pittsburgh area who made their living in the contracting business were eligible to apply for a unique form of college assistance. The NAPCO Aluminum Company in the greater Pittsburgh area was offering a college grant. Applicants were required to answer essay questions about college and their future. Matt by this time had become an expert on essay scholarship applications. He quickly applied and was awarded the scholarship.

Matt Szczypinski and his family are a fine example of how successfully to navigate one's way through the complex labyrinth of college financial aid options. Dealing with college, state, and federal bureaucracies can be confusing, frustrating, and very time-consuming. But in the end, these resources can prove indispensable to you and your family. All that you need are a general understanding of the many options at hand, a close working relationship with the college financial aid office, and a lot of elbow grease. Matt and his family applied and received financial aid from no fewer than six different sources throughout his college career.

A postscript to the Matt Szczypinski story, lest you think he was consumed entirely with filling out financial aid forms: During his 1994 senior year at Washington and Jefferson, Matt's team posted an 11–2 record and played in the Division III national championship. Matt was a three-year starter on the team and capped off his senior year by being named to First-Team All-America by the Associated Press and the Coaches Association. He was most valuable player of the President's Athletic Conference (rare for a defensive tackle) and named to the Eastern Collegiate Athletic Conference All-Star Team. Most significantly, he was named College Division's Defensive Player of the Year (for the entire country) by *College Sport* magazine, a remarkable conclusion to this smart and industrious student-athlete's career.

NCAA **Financial Aid**

Grant-in-Aid

Under NCAA bylaws, student-athletes who have met the proper requirements and are enrolled in a Division I or Division II college may receive athletic financial assistance from the school that includes tuition and fees, room and board, and books. Generally, the type of college scholarship pursued by high school student-athletes is referred to by the NCAA as a "full grant-in-aid." This scholarship is provided by the schools athletic department and covers in full the costs of attending college listed above.

Student-athletes who receive full grants-in-aid related to their athletic ability will be ruled ineligible for this form of financial aid if they receive *any* financial assistance from the school, direct or indirect, beyond the definition of the cost of education. Government-funded Pell Grants, however, available to low-income families, are an exception to this rule. The NCAA currently allows qualified student-athletes to receive up to $2,400 for Division I and up to $1,500 for Division II schools in Pell Grant funds, in combination with their full grants-in-aid. Further, other exempted government grants, such as GI bills and military grants, can supplement an athletic scholarship. The NCAA manual should be consulted for specific information on these exemptions.

Student-athletes receiving NCAA full grants-in-aid also must be aware of limitations regarding employment during their athletic eligibility. The NCAA prohibits a scholarship athlete from receiving income from outside employment during the school years at the Division I level. It does allow employment income to be earned over the Christmas vacation for a limited period of time. This NCAA restriction on employment income is a source of rising debate —one of many—within the college athletic ranks. With multi-billion-dollar TV contracts, such as the recent CBS agreement to televise NCAA basketball, and with college coaches earning millions in sneaker contracts, there is a growing cry in the college ranks for the NCAA to share these revenues with the providing them, the student-athletes themselves.

Although the NCAA administration has stood firm on its resolve not to pay stipends to athletes, many observers feel that at least an increase in peripheral benefits should be made available to students. These benefits would include more leniency regarding outside employment, travel compensation, and increased long-distance phone benefits. While these debates take place, however, there is no room whatsoever for student-athlete violations of the current rules. To do so risks eligibility and loss of financial aid.

Finally, while full grants-in-aid are available only for NCAA Division I and Division II, student-athletes, Division III student-athletes may receive financial aid up to the cost of attendance (i.e., tuition, fees, room, board, course-related books, transportation, and other expenses incidental to attendance), provided such aid is based solely on demonstrated financial need and *not* associated with athletic ability.

Financial Need

Many Division I, II, and III schools offer scholarships based on a candidate's demonstrated financial need. A need-based scholarship is awarded only after a lengthy evaluation of a family's financial situation. Parents are required to respond to a detailed financial aid form (FAF) provided by the College Scholarship Service, an independent evaluation service. Based on a formula, the College Scholarship Service determines each family's level of contribution. This information is then forwarded to the appropriate college for further review. The school then determines a family's need based on the cost of education at that institution. The FAF must be submitted each year for reevaluation, and the financial aid granted will vary as the family's financial status fluctuates.

Financial-need scholarships may pay for only a portion of educational costs and may be combined with other awards and loans to cover the cost of education. The first step is to call the financial aid office of the college and inquire about other forms of available financial assistance.

NAIA Financial Aid

Many NAIA member institutions are committed to providing financial aid to qualified student-athletes. The NAIA *Guide for the College-Bound Student* states that "member institutions shall award no more financial aid to a student-athlete than the actual cost of (1) tuition; (2) mandatory fees, books and supplies required for courses; and (3) based on room and board for the student-athlete only." Contact the NAIA for more specific information on financial aid of member institutions. (See the address in the Appendix.)

NJCAA Grants-in-Aid

As stated in the NJCAA *Handbook,* an "athletic grant-in-aid may be awarded to any student-athlete in recognition of his or her athletic ability provided the student-athlete is admitted to the institution as a regular student." In Division I, the grant-in-aid may consist of a "maximum of tuition and fees, room and board, book and course-related material, and transportation costs one time per academic year to and from the college by direct route."

At Division II institutions, the grant-in-aid may consist of a maximum of tuition and fees. No athletic scholarships of any kind may be awarded to students at Division III institutions. Refer to the NJCAA *Official Handbook and Casebook* for more specific information regarding athletic grants-in-aid. (See Appendix.)

Loans

In the absence of a total athletic or academic scholarship, student-athletes at any institution may turn to a combination of institutional grants and private loans. There are many sources of loans, including privately funded plans as well as government subsidy plans. Some loans are provided for parents, others are made directly to the students.

Generally, loans for education are characterized by reasonable interest rates and lengthy repayment terms. The quite popular Stafford loan, for example, is made directly to the student through a bank recognized as a participant in the plan. The federal government guarantees the loan for the student. As much as $4,000 is available for a given year, and the student does not begin repayment until graduation. In some cases, the loan can be repaid over a ten-year period.

Since there are many loan options to review, the best course of action is to contact the financial aid office of a targeted college or university. The institution will provide information on loans that are available to qualified students matriculating at that particular school. (See the Appendix for a sample letter.)

Summary

Qualified student-athletes can pursue athletic and academic financial aid opportunities at designated member institutions of the three primary governing bodies of college athletics: (1) the National Collegiate Athletic Association (NCAA); (2) the National Association of Intercollegiate Athletes (NAIA); and (3) the National Junior College Athletic Association (NJCAA). The schools offering scholarships within these organizations may offer full athletic or academic scholarships or a combination of an athletic scholarship, a financial need grant, and/or an educational loan package.

Above all, however, the student-athlete must remember that a college athletic career and its obligations do not begin or end when an NCAA full grant-in-aid has been received. If you are the recipient of such a grant, there are continuing criteria for eligibility that must be maintained throughout your career, and there are restrictions on the length of time you may receive the grant. Furthermore, if you are not offered a full grant-in-aid, there are still many ways to cover the cost of your education and enjoy a fulfilling athletic career. Make sure that you are aware of all the options as early as possible during the selection process. Stay in close contact with your recruiter and the college's financial aid office regarding the status of your financial aid applications. Do *not* take for granted the processing of your case. The large number of applications processed by financial aid offices can occasionally result in an application being lost or set aside. It is important to *proactively* check on the progress of your application to ensure fulfillment within your predetermined time lines.

5. Eligibility for Scholarship

The NCAA faces a dilemma. It would like to provide an even playing field for all deserving student-athletes to further their academic and athletic experience. However, even with strict guidelines for eligibility, abuses of the system continue to occur. Clearly, the ultimate goal must be the admission of legitimate students into our educational institutions. The NCAA cannot endorse a system that encourages simply "getting by." The reason colleges and universities exist is *for education*, and athletics must remain a part, and not the whole, of the educational process of the student-athlete. If the student-athlete is to receive an invitation to participate at a member NCAA, NJCAA, or NAIA institution, it must be within the guidelines for eligibility selected by these organizations. All the governing bodies print guidelines for academic eligibility. You are urged to write or call these associations for their respective guides. (See the Appendix for addresses and telephone numbers.) Furthermore, the student-athlete must also meet the college or university guidelines associated with the target school. In some cases, these requirements are more stringent than the NCAA, NAIA, or NJCAA requirements.

In addition to academic criteria for eligibility, the NCAA maintains other standards. The student-athlete is required each year, prior to competing in intercollegiate athletics, to sign a statement that provides information regarding his or her status of eligibility. The athlete must be in compliance with NCAA rules regarding

- Illegal drug use—athletes must agree to testing
- Professionalism—the athlete cannot have accepted payor the promise of pay in any form for participation in his or her sport
- Awards, benefits, and expenses—these types of compensation are strictly regulated
- Ethical conduct, including:
    fraudulent entrance exams
    dishonesty
    prior eligibility under an assumed name
- Unauthorized financial aid
- Illegal recruitment

NCAA Academic Guidelines

The NCAA continues to struggle with the implementation of high school academic standards for college entrance and eligibility. In recent years, the Presidents' Commission of the NCAA has championed a reform movement with regard to these standards. This forty-four-member board of university presidents from across the country has created a sliding scale formula that combines test scores (SAT or ACT) with grade point averages.

Currently, under NCAA guidelines, you must meet the requirements of what is commonly referred to as Proposition 48 to be eligible for an athletic scholarship. Proposition 48 requires the student-athlete to

1. graduate from high school;
2. attain a grade point average of 2.0 (based on a maximum of 4.0) in a successfully completed core curriculum of at least eleven academic courses (See NCAA Guide for the College-Bound Student-Athlete);
3. achieve a 700 combined score on the SAT (Scholastic Assessment Test) verbal and math sections or an 18 composite score on the ACT (Amercian College Test). These test scores must be achieved no later than July 1 immediately preceding the student-athlete's collegiate freshman year.

However, effective August 1, 1996 (by order of new Proposition 16) for those student-athletes first entering col-

legiate institutions on or after that date in Division I, NCAA
Bylaw 14.3 requires a student-athlete to

1. graduate from high school;
2. successfully complete a core curriculum of at least
   thirteen academic courses that includes at least
   three years in English, two in mathematics, two in
   social science, two in natural or physical science
   (including at least one laboratory class, if offered by
   the high school), and two additional courses in
   English, mathematics, or natural or physical science, and successfully complete two additional
   courses in any of the above areas or in a foreign language, computer science, philosophy, or nondoctri-
   nal religion;
3. attain a grade point average (based on a maximum
   of 4.0) and achieve a combined score on the SAT verbal and mathematical sections or a composite score
   on the ACT based on the following index scale:

Core GPA	Minimum SAT	Minimum ACT
Above 2.5	700	17
2.5	700	17
2.475	710	18
2.450	720	18
2.425	730	18
2.400	740	18
2.375	750	18
2.350	760	19

Core GPA	Minimum SAT	Minimum ACT
2.325	770	19
2.300	780	19
2.275	790	19
2.250	800	19
2.225	810	20
2.200	820	20
2.150	840	20
2.100	860	21
2.050	880	21
2.000	900	21
Below 2.000	Not Eligible	

At Division I schools, the minimum required SAT or ACT score must be attained no later than July 1 immediately preceding the individual's first full term in college. At Division II schools, the minimum required SAT or ACT score must be attained prior to the student's first full-time enrollment in college.

It should be noted that freshman-eligibility standards are frequently being reviewed by the NCAA and subject to change. Student-athletes should contact the NCAA directly (see Appendix) for the most current ruling on entrance requirements. Furthermore, prospective student-athletes are required by the NCAA to register with the NCAA initial-elegibility clearinghouse to establish their eligibility credentials.

As a result of increased pressure over these criteria for entrance and eligibility, the NCAA has created two categories of eligibility for incoming freshman: qualifiers and partial qualifiers.

>   Qualifiers are student-athletes who have met all the requirements listed above under Proposition 48 (or Proposition 16, after August 1, 1996).

>   Partial qualifiers in Division I are student-athletes who have not met all the requirements but at the time of graduation from high school have a cumulative grade point average of at least 2.5 (on a 4.0 scale).

>   Partial qualifiers in Division II are student-athletes who have not met all the requirements but at the time of graduation from high school have met either the grade point average criterion or the minimum test score criterion (SAT or ACT).

Qualifiers are immediately eligible for consideration by NCAA member institutions for admission, scholarships and intercollegiate varsity competition. Partial qualifiers are eligible for admission consideration but not for athletics-related scholarships or intercollegiate competition. Partial qualifiers may practice with their team until they attain academic eligibility. Having attained academic eligibility by meeting university and NCAA standards after their freshman year they will have three years of intercollegiate eligibility remaining.

The rules for qualifiers and partial qualifiers are under continual debate and subject to change. You are urged to check with your target institutions for their treatment of the qualifying rules. While the NCAA allows for acceptance of partial qualifiers, many athletic conferences and institutions elect not to accept partial qualifiers.

One argument against the sliding-scale formula of grade point average and test scores is that these criteria unfairly eliminate many minorities and socioeconomically disadvantaged students from eligibility. In fact, opponents of the standardized test score criterion point out NCAA research which shows that 47 percent of black athletes who entered college between 1984 and 1985 (under the lower standards) and went on to obtain their college degrees actually would have been ineligible for admission under the new Proposition 16 guidelines. The influential Black Coaches Association (BCA) considered boycotting NCAA basketball games in 1994 at the height of the debate. The organization later backed away from boycott talk but remains adamant that standardized tests are racially biased.

Proponents believe that student-athletes will benefit from the new requirements. The NCAA cites higher graduation rates among all athletes since the original Proposition 48 standards were instituted in 1982. The Presidents' Commission appears strongly committed to the continual raising of academic standards. However, in response to opposition, the NCAA delayed total implementation from August 1995 to August 1996.

There is little question that academic standards are an important element in maintaining the integrity of collegiate athletics. But at what point do "higher standards" create diminishing returns? When admission requirements for intercollegiate varsity athletes begin to exceed the criteria for other students at the same university, we have lost perspective of the role on sports in education. Imposing extraordinary standards on athletes qualifies intercollegiate sports as an extraordinary element of the educational process. I do not believe that is what the Presidents' Commission really has in mind as its ultimate goal.

As a footnote ,you should know that the NCAA has created a subcommittee on initial-eligibility waivers to grant exceptions to the initial-eligibility requirements. However, all exceptions must be initiated through a member school that has officially accepted the prospect for enrollment. Please refer to the *NCAA Guide for the College-Bound Student-Athlete* for more details on eligibility requirements and waivers (See the Appendix).

NAIA Guidelines

The NAIA *Guide for the College-Bound Student* lists regulations for entrance and eligibility of the student-athlete, who must meet two of three entry level requirements:

1. Score a composite of 15 on the ACT, taken on a national testing date prior to your fall enrollment, or a composite of 18 on the enhanced ACT, taken on a national testing date in October of your fall enrollment, or later on, score 700 combined on the SAT.
2. Achieve an overall high school grade point average of 2.0 on a 4.0 scale.
3. Graduate in the top half of your high school class.

The NAIA guide prints more specific qualifications for entrance requirements and eligibility for athletic grants-in-aid. Refer to the NAIA *Guide for the College-Bound Student* for detailed information regarding eligibility. (See the Appendix.)

NJCAA Guidelines

The NJCAA handbook states that an athletic grant-in-aid may be awarded to any student-athlete provided the student-athlete is admitted to the institution as a regular student. Requirements for entering students include the following:

1. The student must be a high school graduate or attained a high school equivalency diploma, or have been certified as having passed a national test such as the General Education Development Test (GED).
2. Non-high school graduates can establish eligibility for athletic participation by completing one term of college work passing twelve credits with a 1.75 GPA or higher.
3. Non-high school graduates who have earned sufficient credit for high school graduation status can establish eligibility for athletic participation by completing one term of college work passing twelve credits with a 1.75 GPA or higher.

The NJCAA prints more specific qualifications for entrance requirements and eligibility for athletic grants-in-aid. Refer to the NJCAA handbook for detailed information regarding eligibility (See the Appendix.)

6. The Recruiting Process

Imagine what it would be like to receive fifty-five full scholarship offers to play Division I college basketball. That was the position Tyrone Pitt found himself in as he was preparing to graduate from Overbrook Regional High School in Pine Hill, New Jersey, in 1984. The options seem even more incredible when you dig a little deeper and learn more about Tyrone's road to athletic scholarship.

One of ten children born to John and Betty Pitts, Tyrone grew up on the rough streets of Camden, New Jersey. Both parents had not attended high school, and both suffered from physical handicaps. When Tyrone was in the seventh grade, his family was evicted from their home. "You come out of your house and see your things lying on the sidewalk. The feeling that hit me that day was a feeling I never wanted to feel again." Tyrone reflects that "from that day forward I was determined to succeed."

As a result of the eviction Tyrone went to live with his aunt and uncle in Lindenwold, New Jersey. Up to this point in his life, Tyrone had not been a dominant athlete. But just at a time when his desire to succeed intensified, so did his physical development. His real breakthrough came during the last game of his freshman year in high school. He had started for the junior varsity team but sat on the bench for most of the varsity games. Into the final three minutes of the last varsity game, Tyrone scored eight points. He was dubbed "Mr. Excitement" by the local media. The nickname would turn out to be prophetic as Tyrone developed into a three-year varsity starter and was named all-conference player, all-state player, and honorable mention all-american, and he became the leading scorer in Overbrook history.

But as you might guess, that's not the entire story. Before Tyrone graduated from high school, his uncle passed away. Tyrone moved back to Camden with his family, which by now had relocated to a new home. Tyrone did not want to leave his teammates and the success he was experiencing at Overbrook. Consequently, Tyrone decided to commute to Overbrook from his parent's house.

This meant getting up at 5 A.M. every morning and catching the train and two buses needed to make the connection to Lindenwold. The return trip at night was after two to three hours of basketball practice, making for quite a long day.

But Tyrone never stalled in his drive for success and never forgot his father's words of inspiration: "It doesn't matter where you begin, it's where you end up that counts." He also focused on extending his competitive edge in athletics to the classroom. Tyrone was determined that no one would beat him on the court or in the classroom. He was determined to succeed against any odds and at the highest levels. By the end of his senior year in high school, Tyrone Pitts was recognized as the president of the Honor Society, valedictorian of his senior class at Overbrook, and the New Jersey Scholar-Athlete of the Year!

You can imagine why the college coaches and recruiters were all over the six-foot-five guard from Overbrook. Tyrone had a difficult time sorting out the hundreds of "love letters" he received from college basketball coaches. He was impressed by all of the well-dressed and smooth-talking recruiters, who constantly reinforced his ego.

Fortunately, Tyrone had a great deal of help from his high school coaches and administrators during his recruitment. But the process took a toll on his family and his coach. From the fifty-five interested schools they drew up their own list of choices. Even though Tyrone was highly recruited, he still had difficulty deciding at which level to play.

In the end, his final list consisted of three choices, all completely different kinds of schools. Wichita State was a major college power with a superstar: Xavier McDaniel. Northeastern was a "mid major" (a major basketball pro-

gram generally ranked in the middle of Division I) with a
respected coach and a promising freshman, Reggie Lewis.
The University of Pennsylvania was an Ivy League power-
house close to Tyrone's family that had the right level of
play, the Wharton School of Business, and an assistant coach,
Scott Beeten, who was very persistent and convincing.

Coach Beeten had followed Tyrone's development from
the young player's sophomore year at Overbrook.
However, it wasn't until Tyrone's senior year that Beeten
felt he had arrived as a top Division I player. Once Beeten
had seen Tyrone mature into a well-rounded, team-oriented
player, the coach could not let him go. The personal relationship that developed between Tyrone and Coach Beeten
during the recruiting process became the deciding factor.
While Tyrone selected the University of Pennsylvania for
many reasons, the primary one was the trust he developed
in Coach Beeten. In fact, to this day, many years after
Tyrone's graduation, the two remain very close friends.

But when Tyrone arrived at Penn for his freshman year,
he had to start from the bottom. Even with his focused attitude and disciplined approach to academics and athletics,
he was surprised at the adjustments that were required to
make the transition successfully from high school to college.
He learned very quickly that the praise he had received
during the recruiting process was yesterday's news. Tyrone
was now just one of fifteen scholarship athletes competing
for a role in the basketball program. He would have to start
from scratch to earn the respect of his new peers and his
coaches. Even Coach Beeten, who had been so encouraging

to Tyrone, now showed no overt favoritism for his favorite recruit.

Tyrone also felt the pressure academically. Having enrolled at one of the most competitive academic schools in the country, he soon discovered that many of the students came from private high schools and were thus better prepared for a college curriculum. He discovered that the amount of material he was being tested on had significantly increased. Cramming for tests was no longer an option, as it had been in high school.

With some effort, Tyrone made the right adjustments. As a freshman, he was a contributor on Penn's Ivy League championship team, and the following year he became a starter—a role he never relinquished. He scored a career total of 1,301 points and was named to the All-Ivy Second Team his senior year, while averaging 17.4 points and seven rebounds per game. As you might guess, Tyrone was named team captain in his senior season.

On graduation from Penn, Tyrone decided to try to extend his basketball career. While he failed to stick with the Philadelphia 76ers of the National Basketball Association (NBA), he did play for six years on the international professional level. Playing pro ball around the world, he made good money and lived in such places as Europe, Australia, and South America.

But in 1994, Tyrone returned to his roots in the Ivy League. He is now an assistant basketball coach at Cornell University. Scott Beeten helped recommend Tyrone for the job. When Tyrone was introduced at the Penn–Cornell game at the Penn Palestra in Philadelphia, he received a standing ovation, seven years after graduation.

Tyrone is now coaching and recruiting in the same cities and gyms where he achieved so much from such modest origins. His story confirms that while the road to athletic scholarship can be complex, it often produces excellent long-term results.

Tyrone was a gifted player who overcame many obstacles to succeed. He kept his academic world in focus, and that helped open up additional options during his recruiting process. He played by the NCAA rules during this process and steered clear of any college coaches with questionable recruiting tactics.

Developments and Changes in the Recruiting Process

The recruiting of college athletes in its contemporary form began back in the 1920s, when college football began to proliferate on campuses around the country. As the prestige of football, baseball, and, later, basketball rose on campus, so did the desire and need to recruit the best teams. For decades, it has been an accepted fact that a nationally prominent sports team serves as a rallying point for students, alumni, faculty, and friends of colleges everywhere. Winning teams generate a feeling of accomplishment and comradeship that ultimately manifests itself in other ways, namely, financial support.

With the introduction of television to college athletics in the 1950s and 1960s, the opportunity for financial gain through athletics exploded. Television advertisers are quick studies. It soon became clear how much college fans loved watching their favorite teams on TV; television producers and advertisers, in turn, love the fans who watch college athletics. College sports fans tend to be college graduates, with generally higher incomes and higher purchasing power. The television networks were and are more than willing to pay enormous fees to colleges for the rights to broadcast the best teams playing in the biggest games.

In the 1990s, the marketing of college athletics has evolved into a science. "Sports marketers" integrate on-site live events and televised events with advertising plans that include promotions, sweepstakes, television ads, stadium signage, and VIP hospitality. There seems to be no end to the creativity of sports marketers. We are now treated to the Prudential halftime scoreboard, Miller Genuine Moments, and the Red Dog 400 NASCAR race. There also seems to be no limit to the revenues generated by this type of marketing. CBS's current contract to broadcast the NCAA men's basketball tournament will exceed $1 billion over the life of the six-year deal. The NCAA is paid hundreds of millions of dollars from a combination of broadcast and cable networks for college football.

As this money is distributed by the NCAA to participating conferences and schools, it results in enormous individual payouts for the big games. The Fiesta Bowl announced an agreement in 1995 with Frito-Lay that has created the richest postseason game in college football history. The two participating teams will receive approximately

$8.5 million *each*, with another $9 million directed to the college bowl alliance. The alliance includes the Sugar and Orange bowls, and they have teamed up with the Fiesta Bowl to attract the college national championship game on a rotating basis.

The Rose Bowl, historically the highest-paying bowl (prior to the Fiesta announcement), now pays out over $6.5 million to each participating school that makes it to the annual New Year's Day football game. There are a half-dozen other bowls that pay out over $1 million per team for the privilege of being selected as one of the country's elite. But alas, the key to sharing in all this wealth is being selected to participate. There are only about a dozen national-caliber bowls with big payouts in football. So the top twenty-four teams experience the ecstasy, while the other one thousand college football teams stay home for the holidays. In basketball, only sixty-four men's Division I teams are selected for the NCAA basketball tournament from among more than three hundred that compete for the chance to attend the big "party." It has become a very elite club.

The difference between participating in these extravaganzas and staying home—and the resulting infusion or loss of hundreds of thousands of dollars—has a dramatic effect on college athletic departments. Postseason play often means the difference between fiscal stability and financial crisis. Very few college athletic programs are self-sustaining businesses. Unless they regularly enjoy the financial benefits of postseason play, they are dependent on subsidies from their universities. As the cost of education rises and government subsidies to educational institutions decrease, competition for funds at colleges and universities intensifies.

Inevitably, athletic directors and the coaches they hire are under intense pressure to develop teams that will share in the wealth, and *on a regular basis*. There is an old saying in sports that coaches live by: "You're only as good as your last game."

So you can see why the competition to recruit the best players is as intense as ever. Coaches and recruiters are human, and humans sometimes bend the rules. Alumni are well-meaning but sometimes misguided. More and more violations seem to be occurring through the association of alumni. Years ago when alumni had unlimited access to locker rooms and players, manipulation of the recruitment process was usually in the form of the clandestine $50 or $100 bill left in the athlete's locker. Now it takes a different form of rule breaking—offers of credit cards, long-distance phone cards, loans, automobile leases, phony jobs, and paid speaking engagements. One of the more creative techniques shared with me by a former pro teammate, involved an athlete's legitimate job as a waiter in a restaurant. Alumni would frequent the restaurant for dinner and leave $100 tips for $20 dinners.

With this type of behavior going on, the NCAA recognized a long time ago that the system would not remain fair without a set of standards and the ability to enforce the standards. Consequently, as the college athletic sweepstakes have dramatically risen over the years, so the NCAA

efforts to try and control the recruiting environment have
intensified.

NCAA Recruiting Guidelines

The NCAA is the dominant organization setting the standards. The NCAA manual now numbers 512 pages, and one
of the most substantive sections in the book is the chapter
on recruiting. It begins with a definition of when the recruiting process officially starts in a student-athlete's life and
details a complex set of rules and regulations, covering topics from phone calls to insurance policies. Significant topics
for high school athletes include the following.

National Letter of Intent

The National Letter of Intent program was designed to for-
malize the agreement between a student-athlete and the college of choice. In the past, scholarship agreements were
loosely worded and allowed competing colleges occasionally to raid players. Also, colleges would sometimes renege
on scholarship offers that had been extended early in the
recruiting process.

As a solution, the Collegiate Commissioners Association,
a voluntary membership group of the NCAA devised the
National Letter of Intent program. Founded in 1964, the program monitors national letters of intent for conferences in
NCAA Division I, Division II, and independent schools.

When a student-athlete signs a letter of intent, he or
she is committing to attend that school for one full year.
The school likewise is committing an athletic-based schol-

arship to the student for one full year. The agreement between the student-athlete and the school is renewed annually.

If the student-athlete is not admitted to the school due to a lack of academic qualifications, the national letter of intent then becomes invalid, and the student can re-sign with another school. If the student is admitted but later decides not to attend or leaves the school he or she must sit out two years before eligibility is restored. Schools may grant athletes a release from their letter of intent if they so choose.

The case of Corey Simon of Pompano Beach, Florida, is an interesting study of the National Letter of Intent program. Simon was an all-American defensive tackle in high school and was recruited by the best football programs in the country, including those of the University of Georgia and Florida State University.

The NCAA made an inquiry that centered on alleged irregularities during the recruitment of Simon, who signed a national letter of intent with Georgia. Concerned about the NCAA inquiry, Simon asked to be released from his letter of intent to Georgia, indicating that he would prefer to enroll at Florida State. Georgia vehemently denied any wrongdoing during Simon's recruitment, and its athletic director, Vince Dooley, resisted releasing Simon from his letter of intent. With many athletic directors, the granting of a release sets a bad precedent. In the mind of Vince Dooley, Simon had made a commitment that Georgia had accepted in good faith and that should now be honored.

At the same time, Florida State football coach Bobby Bowden stated he would not "recruit" Simon while the young man was still bound by Georgia's letter of intent. However, Bowden indicated he could accept Simon as a walk-on (without scholarship) if the player decided to leave Georgia. Technically, as a walk-on Simon would only have to sit out one year before eligibility was restored. But this was a gray area for both the schools and the NCAA. In the end, Georgia was cleared of any recruiting violations and to his credit Vince Dooley consented to release Corey Simon from his letter of intent even though he was not obligated to do so. Simon was now free to enroll anywhere and sit out only one year.

The National Letter of Intent program attempts to serve both the universities and the student-athletes. A question will always remain, however, as to whether seventeen- and eighteen-year-old student-athletes have the right to change their minds during recruiting or should be held to their commitments.

College Visits

Official Visit means that the college has contacted the recruit and has invited the prospect to visit the campus. In this case, the school pays the recruit's transportation, room, and board, and the visit is limited to forty-eight hours on campus. Each recruit is restricted to one such visit per school, and prospects may visit a maximum of five colleges under the official visit definition.

An *Unofficial Visit* occurs when the prospect pays his or

her own expenses to visit a school. The college cannot pay any expenses associated with such a trip. Prospects are allowed as many unofficial visits as desired.

Summer Camps and All-Star Games

Over the past several years there has been a proliferation of camps and all-star games for high school student-athletes. College recruiters use many of these events as a means to evaluate prospects. However, the NCAA does set limits on when college recruiters can visit these camps and games. If a summer camp is promoting exposure to college recruiters you will want to confirm what sessions of the camp will fall in the "open" period for recruiters.

Also, if you are selected to participate in an all-star game *make sure* the game has NCAA approval. In addition, be aware that the NCAA regulates the types of gifts and awards you can receive from all-star and summer-camp participation. Acceptance of gifts beyond the rules can lead to loss of eligibility.

Contact

The NCAA defines contact as "any face to face encounter between a prospect or the prospect's legal guardian and an institutional staff member or athletics representative during which any dialogue occurs in excess of an exchange of a greeting. Any such face to face encounter that is pre-arranged or that takes place on the grounds of the prospect's educational institution or at the side of organized competition or practice involving the prospect or the prospect's high school, preparatory school, two-year college, or all-star team shall be considered a contact, regardless of the conversation that occurs." *

The NCAA goes on to identify contact periods, evaluation periods, quiet periods, and dead periods for college prospects and recruiters. The contact periods are related to the various competition calendars of each individual sport. They were devised to control the pressure placed on student-athletes during the recruiting process. They were also created to provide schools with smaller recruiting budgets an equal opportunity to contact recruits. The restriction of time and number of visits theoretically keeps larger schools from dominating the time of prospects. Also, recent NCAA legislation has barred all contact by alumni to prospects.

Telephone Calls

Here again, the NCAA has chosen to control the time periods of contact by phone, the number of phone calls, and the representatives cleared to call prospects on behalf of an institution. I have known professional football players who have called high school football prospects, on behalf of their alma maters, from the locker room at halftime during an NFL championship game. Imagine being a high school student-athlete, sitting at home and watching the Super Bowl, who receives a call from the game! You just might start to believe you are something quite special Fortunately, alumni are no longer allowed to contact prospects.

---

*NCAA Manual, 1994-95

Also, college recruiters and coaches used to call prospects from the locker room during their own college games—just to demonstrate how interested they were in a particular "blue chip" prospect. That practice was disallowed by NCAA legislation in 1993.

Offers and Inducements

The NCAA prohibits any unauthorized offerings or gifts to student-athlete prospects. This rule dates back to the days when the division between a professional and an amateur was clear cut: professionals were paid, and amateurs received little more than tuition, room, board, and books.

Most of us are familiar with the sad story of Jim Thorpe and the controversy that surrounded his eligibility for the 1912 Olympics. Thorpe was a college football and baseball star for the Carlisle Institute in Carlisle, Pennsylvania. He went on to win the gold medals in the pentathlon and the decathlon in the Olympics in Stockholm. His records in these events actually stood for sixteen years. But shortly after the Olympics, Thorpe was forced to return his medals. It was revealed that Thorpe had, in fact, played minor league professional baseball on a part-time basis during the summers of 1909 and 1910. Thorpe appealed the ruling on the grounds that he was unaware of the rules and had played baseball with many other "amateur" athletes in baseball who were using false names. The International Olympic Committee ruled that "ignorance is no excuse" and refused to reinstate Thorpe. Eventually, moved by requests from generations of Jim

Thorpe fans, the Olympic movement reinstated his medals in 1982.

Today Thorpe's dilemma would not exist. Times have changed dramatically for "amateur" Olympic athletes. In fact the word *amateur* has all but been removed from the Olympic vocabulary, as olympic athletes today regularly receive gifts, awards, and appearance fees.

But the designation "amateur" for college athletes has so far been strongly preserved. The arguments grow louder for compensating the college athletes who are responsible for generating millions of dollars for their respective colleges. But so far there has been little movement toward compensation beyond tuition, room, board, and books. The NCAA prohibits such inducements as employment for relatives of a prospect; gifts of clothing, cash, or merchandise; loans; and free or reduced housing off campus. In fact, the NCAA prohibits scholarship athletes from obtaining jobs during a school's academic terms. The bottom line here is that prospects cannot receive inducements from institutional representatives. If you are being offered gifts, they are probably beyond the rules and could cost you eligibility later in your career.

Standard Recruiting Forms

During the recruiting process, college coaches and recruiters will mail recruiting forms to student-athletes and their high school coaches. These forms are another tool used by college athletic programs to learn as much as possible about a potential prospect.

While the forms vary from school to school, they all essentially request the same information. It is important for all student-athletes to note that college athletic programs are interested in extracting a great deal more than athletic information through these forms, and that conversations and interviews may follow. When a college or university contemplates a sizable financial investment in a young man or woman, it is seeking an individual who will represent the university positively both on and off the field of competition.

Review these forms (found in the Appendix), and note the interest recruiters are showing in your academics, attitude, and ability to work well with others. Understand the true value of being recognized as a well-rounded student-athlete.

7.   Recruiting Miconceptions

I received my first "recruitment letter" from an NFL team after my sophomore year at Lehigh. Our team had achieved its first winning season in a decade, 8–3, and we had an excellent senior class, including our center, John Hill. John had been selected for All-East and had attracted a great deal of interest from pro scouts. These same scouts, I found, would occasionally say hello to the six-foot two, 180-pound sophomore quarterback who had put up some pretty good numbers in his first year as a starter. So I was not entirely surprised when I received it—a letter from the Washington Redskins.

I was ecstatic! This was even better than the airplane ticket for my recruitment trip. It was almost as good as beating our archrival, Lafayette (but not quite). I must admit, I "accidentally" let a few of my teammates notice the letter in my locker. A number of times it just fell out of my notebook. I was on top of the world.

There was one small detail I, with all my self-professed sports savvy, had overlooked; namely, my backup quarterback, Cliff Eby, the team prankster. Sure enough, Cliff had somehow obtained Redskin stationery and manufactured the letter. Naturally, he alerted the entire team (and campus) of his little scam.

The moral is that during any recruiting process, emotions run quite high. Parents and student-athletes must use caution and good judgment when reviewing all the information flowing to them from recruiters and their institutions. It is very easy for something as innocent as a letter to raise expectations disproportionate to the letter's intent. Jumping to quick conclusions regarding recruiting contacts can sometimes lead to bitter disappointment.

The recruiting process is, at best, a very difficult and stressful period for parents, student-athletes, high school coaches, and the coaching staffs of colleges and universities. The governing bodies of colleges and universities have made great strides in refining the rules and regulations that govern athletic recruiting. It is not a flawless process, but it has produced scores of fulfilling and successful collegiate athletic experiences.

At its worst, however, the process results in inflated expectations, derailed careers, and lost opportunities. The blatant violations in the process are quite often brought to public attention. For the most part, these involve tampering with test scores and the distribution of gifts and favors outside the rules of the NCAA and other governing bodies. But the more subtle abuse, and often the most damaging, exploits misguided student-athlete expectations. Parents and student-athletes unfamiliar with this process can and do misinterpret the enthusiasm generated in their direction by recruiters.

The coaches and recruiters have a difficult assignment. To keep their jobs, coaches must improve their institutions' competitive edge each year through a judicious use of limited scholarship funds. Not all student-athletes they recruit will sign with their school, so they must "recruit" more candidates than there are scholarships available. Each year there is a delicate balance to filling out the roster. Sometimes coaches and recruiters need to keep their second and third choices interested in the event that they may not sign their first choice. If their first choice is slow to commit, others are left dangling.

The most difficult task a parent and his or her student-athlete will have during the recruiting process is determining how serious a recruiter is regarding the student-athlete's candidacy and where that athlete fits in, especially in the unlikely event that *all* the other prospects the school is recruiting sign on with that school.

The NCAA's definition of a recruit is a candidate who has been solicited (through visits, phone calls, letters, etc.) by a representative of a given institution. The view of many coaches is that solicitations through letters, phone calls, visits, and so forth are part of the evaluation process and not a commitment to a scholarship. Only when the coaching staff has completed its in-depth evaluation process and has decided to award a scholarship of some kind to a candidate does that student-athlete become an official recruit in the eyes of that program.

Many parents and their student-athletes misinterpret letters, visits, and phone calls as a confirmation of a college's intentions. In fact, they are only part of the evaluation process and must be kept in perspective. Furthermore, if you have been led to believe you are being "recruited," keep in mind that you may be one of several at your position being considered. Just as students will apply to five or six schools for admission, a college athletics program will often "recruit" five or six prospects at every position. The final confirmation comes only when the scholarship award is actually extended to you for signature.

8.

The Marketing of a Student-Athlete

Whether we realize it or not, our entire lives are spent participating on teams and fulfilling roles on those teams. Different types of teams exist not only in athletics but in businesses and social situations as well, with different tasks and areas of interest. If we learn early in life to recognize and carry out our proper roles in these special interest groups, chances are we will receive a much greater sense of enjoyment and success from our experiences with them.

Every family can, and should, broaden its own student-athlete's opportunities for an athletic scholarship. In effect, this involves the marketing of the student-athlete. Any time you expose yourself to a greater number of options, you increase your chances of finding what it is you are seeking. In the selection of a college or the pursuit of a scholarship, this is no different. The more colleges you visit or review, the better your chances of selecting the right one for you. Increase the number of athletic programs that are aware of your skills and potential and you increase your chances for an athletic grant.

There is, however, a real danger when it comes to self-promotion. The challenge for student-athletes and parents alike is to never lose sight of their commitment to the team concept. Good judgment needs to be exercised, and a team member should never be promoted at the expense of the team. Avoid projecting yourself as a "me first" athlete, but do actively project yourself to college coaches.

The NCAA *Guide for the College Bound Student-Athlete* states that "you become a prospective student-athlete" when you are playing on a high school team and have started classes for the ninth grade. It is, of course, very rare for the recruiting process to begin as early as the ninth grade. Colleges are aware of only the most gifted athletes as ninth graders. Most scholarship athletes are identified by colleges in their junior year of high school, and many decisions on awarding scholarships are not made until the senior season of high school competition.

But this does not mean you should wait until your senior season for exposure. Quite the contrary, since the earlier recruiters are exposed to a potential scholar-athlete, the better chance one has of being completely and fairly evaluated.

Therefore, a proactive response to the recruiting process is highly recommended.

Colleges and universities spend a great deal of money every year on recruiting in an effort to locate and sell the best qualified athletes available on their athletic programs. Parents of prospective student-athletes can also contribute to this process.

Important Steps

1. *Develop a close relationship with the high school coach.*

High school coaches are usually sincerely interested in the development of their student-athletes. The relationship between the coach and student-athlete can and should be a special one. The first and most important factor a college recruiter recognizes is not the number of touchdowns, goals, wins, or record times; it is the high school coach's recommendation. A positive relationship between the coach and the student-athlete will produce positive results during the recruiting process.

As noted earlier, if the relationship between the coach and the student-athlete is strained, it could hurt the recruiting process. Intervention by well-meaning parents in coach–student-athlete disputes is strongly discouraged. Even if the parents are right, the student-athlete still loses. For better or worse, the student-athlete must usually live with the coach for his or her entire high school career. The parent must exercise restraint when confronted with what appears to be a negative situation. A coach's relationship with an athlete often will publicly appear antagonistic, while privately it is much stronger. In many cases, parental intervention will not have a positive impact on the coach's final evaluation as submitted on a recruiting form.

The majority of high school coaches take pride in playing significant roles in the college placement of their charges. However, a small minority adamantly maintain that their job starts and stops with coaching and that chasing college scholarships and opportunities is not their responsibility. Any coach who is not interested in doing everything possible for the continuing development of his or her students is misrepresenting the coaching profession. Coaches are in very powerful positions when it comes to a student-athlete's future, and we need to find ways to hold them accountable for their actions or their lack therein.

In sum, parents should demonstrate a great deal of support but keep their distance. They should obtain from the coach a qualified opinion on the potential of the athlete and on the level of competition that may be appropriate. High school coaches receive feedback from college recruiters and should share that information with the parents.

2.   *Parents and student-athletes should contact potential colleges and universities on a proactive basis.*

As the student-athlete begins to identify target schools, it is in his or her best interest to contact the school and coaching staffs and advise them of the student-athlete's interest. This is allowed under NCAA rules and is a good way to attract attention and get on recruiting lists. Most Division I schools have individual sports recruiters. Call the school's athletic department and ask for the office of the individual in charge of recruiting for the appropriate sport. Then compose a brief letter identifying the student-athlete by name, high school, sport and position. (See the Appendix.) Indicate that the student has an interest in the school's program and would appreciate more information at the appropriate time.

Early in this process (grades 10 and 11), you should target schools with varying levels of athletic competition, academic requirements, and social conditions. You should create a spectrum of potential options that range from very challenging programs to ones that are less so.

At this point, keeping options wide open is important. Throughout a student-athlete's high school career, the emphasis should be placed on the enjoyment of the sport and as little as possible on the stress of recruiting. Contacts to and from schools should be enjoyed but not overemphasized.

The NCAA allows only five subsidized, official recruitment trips to college campuses. To receive five invitations, you may have to be contacted by dozens of schools. Therefore, the more colleges that are exposed to the student-athlete, the greater chance of an award.

3. *Make a highlight film.*

Some colleges require films of athletes in their recruiting process. This is most often true in football and basketball. The parent should produce a highlight videotape of the student-athlete if at all possible, to be mailed to recruiters at appropriate schools. A highlight video should be produced as early as the student-athlete's high school career permits. Ideally, it is not just a game film but an edited version featuring the student-athlete's performance in a number of games. Do not simply edit in big plays. Recruiters and coaches like to see overall performance over several games, so edit in at least half of the athlete's best two or three games, if they are available. High schools usually tape games and should share these tapes for reproduction. If necessary, tape your own games. When preparing a tape for distribution, narrow your scope of prospective schools but still be prepared to send tapes to as many as ten or more. Send the tape by registered mail to the appropriate recruiter or coach. (Do not expect the tape to be returned.)

4. Send "updates."

As the student-athlete enters competition in the junior year of high school, begin to send "updates" on his or her athletic and academic progress to schools on your target list. An update should highlight recent athletic achievements and serves as a mechanism to keep the athlete on the minds of coaches and recruiters. (See the Appendix for an example of a student-athlete update.)

5. Measure the feedback from the distribution of your updates and films (when appropriate).

Many coaches are considerate enough, after reviewing their report, to mail out specific feedback on prospects. Some schools will inform you by mail that they have no interest in recruiting your student-athlete. Such responses can be very helpful in narrowing choices and should not be considered simply as rejections. In basketball, for example, a college may have only two or three scholarships to award in a given year. A student-athlete may be a point guard, and the school may not be recruiting a point guard that year. Any feedback from a school is information you can put to good use. However, because recruiting resources are under a great deal of pressure, expect very little feedback—even (or especially) from major colleges.

6. *Attempt to secure a personal visit.*

As your choices narrow and graduation draws closer, try to contact the athletic programs high on your list in order to secure a personal visit. If the athletic department at one university is not cooperative in arranging a personal visit for the student-athlete, move your priorities to the next school on your target list. If no schools are showing scholarship interest, inquire about "walk-on" possibilities, and continue to market the student-athlete as a walk-on candidate if the financial situation is appropriate.

The marketing of a student-athlete should consist of a measured attempt to establish and maintain proactive, informative contact with colleges and coaching staff. There is a systematic process with critical time lines for enhancing a student-athlete's chances of obtaining an athletic scholarship. In every case, the student-athlete's chances are greatly increased if the marketing efforts originate with the high school coach. His or her support, cooperation, and management of the process is crucial to success. Without the coach's participation, the student-athlete's odds for success are greatly diminished.

Parents and student-athletes should make every effort to work with the high school coaches and administrators. In the absence of cooperation, the parents and students can and should press on with a plan of their own. Even in the face of resistance or disinterest, I strongly recommend continual attempts at communication and the establishment of a joint effort by the student-athlete, parents, and coaches.

9.　　　　The Final Decision

Almost six million young men and women compete in varsity high school athletics across America. Of this number, fewer than 5 percent will move on to further their athletic careers at the collegiate level. Furthermore, fewer than one-half of college student-athletes compete at the NCAA Division I level of competition.

The most important aspect of the student-athlete's experience at the collegiate level is the *quality* of the experience, not the level of competition. It is very important for high school student-athletes to identify the right fit academically, athletically, socially, financially, and geographically.

All these factors will determine the degree of success you experience in college and in college athletics. If all these areas are considered and made the most of, then there is a good chance your student-athlete experience will have a positive effect on your development for years to come.

Many successful student-athletes will experience successes and the thrill of testing their potential to the limit at the Division II and Division III levels. Many will carry with them lessons and joys shared with teammates at NAIA schools and at the junior college level. Size alone will sometimes prevent a great athlete from performing at an NCAA Division I school. Rather than pursue an unrealistic goal at Division I, which many times ends in an unfulfilling experience, the same student-athlete might well find his or her potential at a more realistic level. The final decision should not necessarily focus on scaling the highest peak; arriving breathless and spiritually exhausted at the top is not always the right goal. More important, the student-athlete should seek out the mountain with his or her name on it.

College sports are defined by great traditions and great rivalries. In football, Georgia and Georgia Tech compete for bragging rights across the state, Texas and Oklahoma compete in the "Red River Shoot-Out" and the games where Michigan squares off against Ohio State have been sold out for decades. Even professional sports teams have developed heated rivalries, such as the Dodgers versus the Giants and the Yankees versus the Red Sox in baseball. In the NFL, I participated in the always intense Falcons-versus-Saints contests and in games between the archrival

Washington Redskins and Dallas Cowboys. However, surprising as it may seem, the most exciting three games of my
eighteen year athletic career occurred on the Division 1-AA
playing field at Lehigh University. All three games were
against archrival Lafayette College.

Lehigh and Lafayette share the distinction of having
participated in the most frequently played rivalry in the history of college football. These two teams have met over 125
times since 1890. The game has never been carried by a
major television network. The respective school stadiums
hold fewer than twenty thousand fans. The outcome of the
Lehigh–Lafayette game has not had an effect on the national championship since the 1930s. Many college football fans
are not even aware of each school's programs, much less of
a rivalry between the two.

But to the participants, fans, and alumni, it is the biggest
sporting event of the year. It is the game that caps the season, and played as the final game each year, it also is the
final game of the graduating seniors' college career. The
excitement, pressure, and exhilaration are every bit as
intense as if the athletes were playing in the Super Bowl.
Every participant in the Lehigh–Lafayette game is creating
a memory that lasts a lifetime.

The point is that the special experiences of athletic competition abound throughout America. The most important
task is to find your own athletic niche, invest energy in your
athletic pursuits, and achieve a return on your investment.
The level of competition is not the reward; the competition
itself is the reward, and a building block for your future.

For parents, identifying a son or daughter as a legitimate candidate for an athletic scholarship is difficult at best. In the formative, developmental years (grades 9 through 12), student-athletes need positive reinforcement and support. The burdens placed on student-athletes can be significant in terms of scheduling, fatigue, social sacrifices, and emotional stress. Strong, supportive parents can be vital to the degree of success realized by the student-athlete.

But parents have an additional obligation that requires a unique perspective: namely, the application of realistic goals for their student-athletes. We all want our children to strive to fulfill their potential. But the key to a successful athletic experience is realizing the level of that potential. Not everyone can play at the Division I level; in fact, most cannot. Realizing this, and not putting excess pressure on yourself or your child, is crucial.

10.　　　　　　　　　The Walk-On

Jen Smith started playing basketball in the third grade, in a Saturday-morning recreational league in Victor, New York. Jen usually played on boys' teams, where she would hold her own. She didn't realize she was an exceptional player until she started playing on girls-only teams and began to dominate. But Jennifer was an unusually gifted athlete, and it wasn't only basketball that captured her attention.

Jen loved to compete at anything. By the time she was ready to graduate from Victor High School in 1991, she had lettered in varsity soccer, varsity softball, and varsity basket-ball. But Jen didn't just compete; she excelled. She was named to First-Team All-Conference in soccer, Second-Team All-Conference in softball, and Second-Team All-Conference in basketball, and was a member of her region's Amateur Athletic Union (AAU) national tournament team.

And Jen did not limit her achievements to athletic competition. She enjoyed competing in the classroom and getting involved in extracurricular activities. Jen was coeditor of the school newspaper her senior year at Victor, as well as the Girls Leaders Club treasurer, vice president of the Spanish Club, and a member of the National Honor Society. She graduated as the valedictorian of her class.

Jen had always dreamed of playing college sports. Her high school basketball coach was very supportive and even helped Jen put together a highlight tape for college recruiters. You can imagine the surprise and disappointment when college recruiters failed to respond. It appeared that Jen had the complete package, but something seemed to be lacking. Perhaps it was size: she was five-foot eight. Or perhaps it was speed and strength. At any rate, no athletic scholarship offers were extended to her in any sport.

Keep in mind that women's college athletics have traditionally been underemphasized. Although great strides have been made to open up opportunities for women, women's college athletic programs still suffer from a lack of scholarships and recruiting money. Consequently, good prospects like Jennifer Smith can easily be overlooked or left out. This is also true for men in sports that are commonly defined as "nonrevenue" sports, those sports that do not generate positive cash flow through either ticket sales or sponsorship. Some typical nonrevenue sports include men's and women's swimming, golf, cross-country, and tennis; men's wrestling, lacrosse, and baseball; women's softball and field hockey.

Jen decided she was not going to be a victim of the numbers game. She created a plan to visit schools with basketball programs (her favorite sport) but make her decision on the academic and social merits of each school. That way, if her walk-on attempt failed (and odds were that it would), she would be at a school that fulfilled her other needs.

Reviewing her choices, she contacted the coach at Colgate University in Hamilton, New York. Colgate is a fine academic university of about three thousand undergraduates and competes at the Division I level in women's basketball—certainly a challenge for a potential walk-on.

Colgate's coach, Liz Feeley, was interested in Jen but could not offer her a scholarship. Jen was not dissuaded by Coach Feeley's response. One of Jen's older high school teammates had gone to Colgate and was participating in the basketball program. The former teammate gave Feeley high marks as a coach, and Jen believed she could make a positive contribution to the Colgate program if given a chance.

Coach Feeley agreed to accept Jen into the program as a walk-on. All the players on the team were scholarship players except Jen. Jen wondered what kind of a chance she would get to impress the coach and make an impact on the program.

When practice opened up at Colgate during her freshman year, Jen was surprised and delighted to find herself on equal footing with the scholarship athletes. She was given an opportunity to participate, and she made the most of it. Jen started eighteen games as a freshman and averaged 7.3 points and 3.3 rebounds. She was among the league leaders in free throws (.719) and was sixth in assists (3.33 per game).

From her walk-on position as a freshman, Jen's career continued to soar. She ended her career at Colgate as a four-year starter and was team captain in her junior and senior seasons. She was named the Patriot League's most outstanding player three times. She finished her career as the all-time leading scorer in league play, with 1,537 points. She is at or near the top in the Colgate record books for her free-throw percentage (.721), field goal percentage (.439), scoring average (14.2), rebounding (616), and steals (201). Jen was named Patriot League Female Scholar-Athlete in her senior year. She was later named First Team Academic All-American and was a regional finalist for a Rhodes Scholarship.

Jennifer Smith defied the odds and came out a winner. But she was able to accomplish what she did by keeping all aspects of her college career in perspective from the beginning. She selected a walk-on opportunity that met the criterion of both the school and the program satisfying her needs beyond athletics. Colgate would have provided an excellent home for Jen without basketball in the equation. She targeted an environment that was good for her other needs, and that approach provided her with the comfort and confidence to succeed.

Athletes who attempt to participate in college athletics without the benefit of being recruited and awarded an athletic scholarship are frequently referred to as "walk-ons," because they are walking onto the program without the formal invitation of a scholarship offer. Almost all schools need walk-ons to fill out their athletic rosters. In the high-revenue sports, such as basketball and football, walk-ons are used in practice sessions and very rarely get an opportunity to play in a game or even to suit up in the uniform on game day. It is largely a support role and requires an unselfish approach to participation. The walk-on must identify benefits to participating in the program apart from actual game participation. In some cases, it can be very fulfilling simply to know you are playing a contributing role as part of a college athletic program. Peripheral benefits include camaraderie, expanding your knowledge of the sport, experiencing the discipline and sacrifice, and developing a network of friends, coaches, and alumni associated with the program.

Traditionally, nonrevenue sports have relied to a great degree on walk-on participation, in practice and in actual games. Many sports such as baseball, soccer, swimming, lacrosse, field hockey, and so forth do not have the funds available to recruit or award scholarships to every team member. Consequently, a student-athlete may walk-on to these sports knowing there is a higher chance of game-day participation.

There are really two categories of walk-ons. The first involves a student-athlete who has never been contacted by the targeted athletic program and is really walking on without any encouragement from the college coach. The odds of success in this situation are very slight.

The second type of walk-on role is preferred. The college athletic department is aware of the student-athlete prior to freshman enrollment and has encouraged the student to walk on. Some schools refer to this category as a "preferred walk-on." For example, at some schools a preferred walk-on in basketball will not only be invited to try out but may be guaranteed a spot in the program for the duration of the student-athlete's college career. The athlete will practice and dress for games with the team and possibly play in games. The walk-on is not on scholarship, but if the athlete produces, he or she may have the opportunity to be awarded a partial or full scholarship for the remaining years of eligibility.

Preferred walk-on status is generally achieved in one of two ways. In the first scenario, the college recruiter or coach has scouted the prospect and wants to invite the student-athlete into the program. Because the program does not have a scholarship available for this athlete, they invite the prospect into the program as a walk-on. The second scenario involves a student-athlete who has identified a university as a high priority on his or her list (academically, socially, geographically, etc.) and contacts the athletic office regarding walk-on status. It is always an advantage for the student-athlete to solicit the high school coach's recommendation if the athlete intends to apply as a walk-on candidate. In fact, in many cases the high school coach makes the contact for the student-athlete. Ideally, the contact is made early enough for the college to have time to scout the walk-on in actual competition or film.

There are several areas of concern regarding walk-on candidacy. First and foremost, *it is most probable that you will never receive an athletic scholarship*. You should enter the college and athletic program with a plan based on not receiving athletic financial aid. The athletic department should be helpful, however, in directing you to financial aid available to the general student body. Next, it is very important, albeit difficult, that you *attempt to measure your value to the coach and his program*. Most coaches are sincere recruiters and will give you an honest appraisal of your walk-on value to the athletic program. But there are always exceptions whose attitude is that the more competition they have in their preseason periods, the better the team. They have little or no intention of keeping some walk-ons beyond a point that is helpful to them. You may therefore receive a verbal promise that remains unfulfilled.

The best way to measure the sincerity of a coach or recruiter is by asking pointed questions and relying on your instincts to evaluate the sincerity of the answers. A good backup, however, is to get the answers to your questions from more than one source. If an assistant coach has been your contact, ask to speak to the head coach as well. Also, confirmation from the athletic director's office can be most helpful. Do not hesitate to ask the coach for a letter describing the terms of your walk-on candidacy. Most coaches will not accommodate a walk-on in writing, but an explanation of why a coach will not provide such a letter might lend insight to your evaluation.

Finally, keep in mind that *scholarship student-athletes in the program will be exposed to benefits not available to walk-on candidates.* Such benefits include not only the actual scholarship but also training-table food programs and residence in the athletic dorm or preferred housing status, as well as other, extra benefits. Be prepared to assume a low-profile, high-sacrifice role as a walk-on.

There are countless stories in college athletics of walk-on candidates like Jen Smith who rose above the fray to the highest levels of success. It takes a strong–minded, well-focused student-athlete to experience a successful walk-on career. Some walk-ons—very few—achieve an athletic scholarship, a starting position, and even, on rare occasions, All-America status. Anything is possible. More realistically, however, the achievement is successful participation as a member of an intercollegiate varsity team and the maturity to recognize that such an experience, even as a support member of the team, will benefit the student-athlete for a lifetime. Always remember, the level of participation is not nearly as important as taking on the challenge and developing the discipline to see it through.

11. The High School's Role: How To Build Your Plan

As we mentioned earlier, of the five million plus high school varsity athletes, only about a quarter of a million will go on to compete at the college varsity level. A very small percentage of these athletes are identified in high school as "can't miss" prospects. The highly publicized early signers are very rare. The remaining student-athletes arrive at their college destination from a wide range of avenues. Some are discovered by college scouts, while others are promoted and introduced to college recruiters by friends, family, or their high school coaches. Many are not recognized in high school as future college stars, but they have set a goal and are determined to reach it.

All young people need a reason to feel special about themselves. With some students, this involves excelling in math, English, or a foreign language; with others, it may be the result of playing a musical instrument or participating as a member of the student council. If you are reading this book, chances are your special niche is athletics. Athletics is your edge in the marketplace when it comes to selling yourself. The proper use of that edge by the high school can make a difference in building a student-athlete's future.

In discussing this subject with college coaches, I am no longer surprised to hear how many high school athletic programs do little or nothing to promote their deserving student-athletes. Like many parents, the high schools view their role as passive or do not even recognize a role exists.

The process for student-athlete college placement is extraordinarily competitive for scholarship and even walk-on candidates. In this business, a delayed response is a lost opportunity. If the high school or its coach is unresponsive to calls, letters, and visits from college recruiters, a student-athlete can get pushed down a college's priority list very quickly, and these lists are very long.

High schools can and should develop a plan for the growth and placement of their student-athletes. While such a plan will vary from sport to sport, there are some basic guidelines that can be followed by high school coaches and administrators in most varsity sports. Building a plan may seem a formidable task at first, but its systematic implementation can take place over a one- or two-year period, and once it is established, it becomes easy and fulfilling to maintain.

How to Build Your High School Plan

Athlete Counseling

Every high school varsity coach should meet once a year
with their athletes to determine the athletes' ambitions and
goals for the high school and collegiate levels. For most athletes, the counseling should begin by the sophomore year in
high school. The counseling session should consist of a private, one-on-one meeting between the athlete and the
coach. Many young student-athletes consider lofty athletic
ambitions a very personal and even embarrassing subject.
The coach should emphasize that the session is entirely con-
fidential. The coach should target three general areas of dis-
cussion:

1. Where are you today as an athlete? This should
   include an honest appraisal of the athlete's dedica-
   tion and performance to date.
2. What are your goals in athletics at the high school
   level, and what must you do to achieve these goals
   by your senior year? This includes developing a
   personal game plan for growth and development.
3. Do you have an interest in competing at the collegiate level, and if so, what level should you target as
   a goal? The important message is that fulfillment can
   be found at all college levels of athletic competition.

The coach must always remember that dreams are usually the first step to a fulfilling athletic career. The most dif-

ficult task any high school coach faces is managing the
dreams of his pupils. If the student-athlete identifies college
athletics as a goal, then the counseling will serve as the basis
for designing a realistic road map to reach that goal. Any
student-athlete identifying such a goal should also be reminded that extraordinary focus and commitment are needed
to advance to the next level.

Talent, of course, plays a major role in any student-athlete's ability to compete in college. Certainly, when counseling a student-athlete, the coach must factor in his or her own
subjective evaluation of the athlete's potential. However,
focus, commitment, and a desire on the part of the athlete to
sacrifice may play just as important roles in the evaluation.
Coaches should always bear in mind that sophomores and
juniors are capable of rapidly maturing and significantly
improving their athletic evaluation from one year to the
next. The key ingredient may be desire. College athletic programs are filled with overachieving athletes who were
labeled too slow or too small. Coaches should always measure the heart first.

In the final analysis, the high school is not required to
make a final determination on the athletic potential of its
student-athletes. College coaches and recruiters are professionals at evaluating talent and potential. It is not the
high school's responsibility to recommend student-athletes for scholarship. The high school's role should be
to ensure that its deserving student-athletes have the best
possible opportunity to be evaluated by the professionals.

Preparation

1.   Physical conditioning

Once it has been established that a student-athlete has a strong, sincere desire to advance his or her athletic career beyond high school, the work really begins. An integral part of the high school coach's counseling should be an evaluation of the athlete's physical strengths and weaknesses. A standard off-season and summer workout routine should be created for all athletes who are interested in improving their level of achievement. While the specific type of workout will vary from sport to sport, any program should target improving strength and overall conditioning.

2.   Off-season camps and special events

Spring and summer camps are becoming an integral part of the recruiting process. This is especially true in football, basketball, soccer, wrestling, and baseball. The NCAA gives college recruiters specific times during the year to visit and evaluate prospects. Consequently, hundreds of camps have sprung up during these open evaluation periods. The camps are generally found on college campuses and are staffed by high school coaches.

Camps can be very good for athletes, but they can be very bad for them as well. Most camps are usually high on competition and low on teaching. The best camp is one that exposes the athlete to good competition but also provides qualified instructors for the teaching segments. Many camps promote appearances by college and pro celebrities, but usually these are very brief visits at the camp. Try to focus on camps that concentrate on teaching and exposure, not camps high on hype.

If a high school coach is interested in recommending a camp for his or her athletes, the coach should ask:

- Is the camp being run by a college athletic department or by an outside organization or individual?
- How many competitors are expected to attend, and in what age brackets?
- How many instructors or coaches will participate per athlete, and what is their experience level?
- How many college recruiters or coaches attended last year's camp, and how many are expected this year?
- Does the camp provide an evaluation program of its athletes, and are the evaluators qualified?
- Are the camp fees competitive with other camps? (Generally, camps will run from $200 to $300 for a five-day, overnight camp, including all meals.)
- Will the camp provide evaluation reports to college recruiters?
- Will the camp share the report with the student-athlete?

3.   Academics

The student-athlete should be briefed early in high school regarding the NCAA, NAIA, and other college associations' academic rules for scholarship eligibility. Early identification of academic requirements can provide incentives to student-athletes to perform better in the classroom. (See chapter 5.)

College Contacts

There are a number of ways in which a high school can make its campus a user-friendly environment for college coaches and recruiters and also provide important information on its varsity athletes.

1.   College file

Coaches in individual varsity sports should begin to build a file of athletic programs at the college, junior college, and prep school levels. The file should include updated information including each college coach's name, address, and phone number. It would also help to categorize the schools academically and become familiar with their general entrance requirements.

2.   Letter of introduction

The high school coach should have a standard letter of introduction on file and available for student-athletes in the varsity program. The letter should identify the athlete, the high school, the level of competition, team and individual accomplishments, and, when appropriate, a personal letter of recommendation from the coach.

3.   Fact sheets

The high school should instruct athletes, coaches, and parents on the development of athlete fact sheets. These are periodic updates sent after the initial letter of introduction. A fact sheet should provide colleges on the student-athlete's target list with information regarding the progress of the athlete. (See the Appendix.)

4.   Films and videotapes

Colleges require videotapes of student-athletes in many scholarship sports. High schools are often slow to respond to film requests from parents and colleges, usually because they have only one film that must be shared. Also, quite a few parents are reluctant or intimidated to request game films. A formal, open film policy should be adopted by the school.

In fact, films could be a source for booster-club fund-raising. Send notification to all varsity players and cheerleaders that films are available for sale; the proceeds go to the booster clubs. Regardless of the student's interest in college athletics, I am certain most parents would want at least one film for posterity.

Requests from a college for a film should be filled immediately. Any delay could be very harmful to the recruiting process. College athletic programs will generally return a film, but many do not. Waiting on the return of a film to fulfill additional requests could cause severe delays. Parents should expect to pay for additional film requests.

5.   Visitation

Encourage the student-athlete and parents to get out and visit colleges. NCAA rules permit visits to college games, and the colleges are usually very eager to provide tickets. This gives the athletes and the parents a firsthand view of the intensity of play at the collegiate level.

6.   Communication

High school coaches should promptly share college contact letters, phone calls, and requests with the student-athlete and the parents. I am amazed by how many high school coaches withhold information to prevent their athletes from getting "big heads." The school has an obligation to share feedback from colleges on student-athlete's progress and growth.

7.   Public Relations

High school coaches, athletic directors, and/or administrators should develop a rapport with any local sportswriters who cover their teams. Call them up and thank them for the coverage. Advise them of your willingness to cooperate with them and provide information. College coaches and recruiters do read newspapers and magazines—use it to your advantage.

Also, keep accurate statistics and check league and/or county listings to make sure they accurately reflect the performance of your athletes. At the same time, high schools can provide writers with stories on unique student-athletes in their programs.

Placement

Make sure your student-athletes are properly counseled on creating a target list of colleges prior to the senior year. The athletes, like the entire student body, should be counseled on admission procedures and applications. Most college recruiters advise their college admissions office of recruits who have filed applications. This notification can positively effect the admissions process.

Attempt to receive feedback from college recruiters on student-athletes. Recruiters are likely to be more straightforward with a high school coach than with a parent or an athlete. Share this information with student-athletes and parents, so that everyone maintains realistic expectations.

Build a Legacy

It is a great asset to stay in touch with former high school student-athletes who have successfully graduated to the collegiate level. These dynamic alumni can help keep their personal collegiate contacts focused on their high school alma mater. College coaches recognize talented high school programs and enjoy building relationships with these programs. High schools should make an effort to keep the lines of communication open.

Former players should be encouraged to visit and welcomed back to the high school campus. High schools could even feature their athletic legacies at pre-game or halftime events. These young success stories also often make fine speakers at postseason award banquets and fund raisers.

12. Important Questions

Twenty Important Questions to Ask of College Coaches and Recruiters

1. How many of your student-athletes in my sport obtain their degrees within four years? Within five years?

In ensuring your academic and athletic success, a key objective must be a quality education and your athletics department's commitment to your graduation. Many schools measure their graduation success by how many students have graduated five years from entering school. If graduation rates are below 50 percent after five years, you must question the program's commitment to your education. If a school has high graduation rates in a four-year period, the program clearly emphasizes academic, as well as athletic, performance.

2. *How does the graduation rate for student-athletes compare to that of the entire student body?*

Comparing athlete graduation rates to those of the general student body is a strong way of indicating how seriously the school strives to keep athletics in perspective. Ideally, the two figures should be very close.

3. *Will my financial assistance cover my education through four years and beyond, if necessary?*

If a school tells you it is extending you a "full" scholarship, a key question is, For how long? If many of a college's athletes are taking five or more years to graduate, will the grant support the student-athlete through to graduation. The answer to this should be stipulated *in writing*.

4. *Under what conditions might my financial assistance be revoked?*

All financial aid requires students to meet academic as well as behavioral requirements. Student-athletes must demonstrate progress toward graduation; if they do not, they are subject to academic probation or worse. Student-athletes need to know the status of financial aid during probationary periods. The NCAA, the conferences, and individual schools vary on this issue. Some schools will continue to provide financial aid if the student-athlete experiences academic problems, while other schools may withdraw aid under certain circumstances. Get a *clear* understanding from your recruiter of *all* the restrictions on financial aid that may apply to you.

5. *What position and role does the school foresee for me in its athletic program?*

It is a good idea to get a clear understanding of how the coaching staff sees you fitting into the program. If you were a quarterback in high school, do they plan on playing you at quarterback or moving you to another position? If you were a medium- and long-distance track star in high school where does the college program see you excelling? If you were a two-sport athlete in high school will participation in both sports be allowed by your college program? In many cases, college recruiters recruit "athletes" and not position or role players. They may be excited by your athletic ability and have little or no intention of playing you at your high school position. The change may suit the student-athlete just fine. But as in marriage, these details should be discussed openly among the student-athlete, parents, and coaches prior to a commitment.

6. *How many other athletes at my position does your school intend to sign?*

This is a fair question to ask of any college coach. You can expect stiff competition on the collegiate level in any sport, so try to get a general idea of how deep the team will be at your position, in terms of both current players and new recruits.

7. *What are the year-round requirements of participants in my sport?*

College athletics has become big business. The NCAA is trying hard to provide student-athletes with a reasonable amount of free time during season, as well as in the off-season, but you should be prepared for a full-time, year-round commitment to sports once you're at the college level. However, you should inquire about the details. Find out whether your program requires double sessions in the off-season beginning at 5:15 A.M. or workouts on your own.

8. *Does the athletic department or university provide access to or assistance with summer jobs?*

While it is against NCAA rules for scholarship athletes to hold jobs during the school year, it is permissible to obtain employment during the summer months. Many colleges provide job placement information for summer employment. A summer job for a student-athlete that falls within the guidelines of NCAA rules can go a long way toward offsetting extraordinary expenses that are not covered by the athletic scholarship.

9. *Does your school redshirt athletes?*

At many universities the athletic program has the option to "redshirt" an athlete, that is, hold the athlete out of competition for a year with no loss of eligibility. Usually this is done to allow the athlete to mature (athletically and/or academically). Some schools have a policy against redshirts. Find out what the school policy is on redshirting and inquire in advance whether they intend to redshirt you.

10. *Does your scholarship cover the costs of health care on and off the field of competition?*

Most athletic scholarships cover injuries incurred during the course of your sports participation. They also generally cover all costs associated with any long-term rehabilitation. But schools have varying policies about general health care costs. Many schools require additional coverage for non-sports related health care benefits. Inquire about the extent to which you, as a student-athlete, will be covered.

11. *What are the living arrangements for student-athletes?*

Some universities provide special housing for athletes, perhaps in a special section of a dormitory or in a completely segregated dorm, for athletes only. Other schools prefer to integrate their athletes and have them experience the school as a resident of the regular student housing. Also, inquire about any changes in housing provisions as a result of academic probation or discipline. Athletes may lose athletic dorm privileges if their academic status falls under probation.

12. *What are the meal-plan arrangements?*

Most college athletic programs provide some type of special meal program for their student-athletes. Sometimes the meal program is limited to one meal a day or only during the season. Other programs provide all meals, year-round.

13. Is academic tutoring available for student-athletes? Is there a charge?

Tutoring programs exist at most schools for the general student body. Student-athletes, given the added demands on their time, may occasionally require a tutor. Inquire if the athletic department will provide tutors for you as needed, and if there is a charge.

14. How are athletic and academic conflicts treated at the university?

During the course of four years, it is inevitable that practices, games, and classes will occasionally conflict. Ask your coach which comes first and how difficult it is to make up work. Will you be disciplined by the coach for missing a practice because of an afternoon lab?

15. Will I have the freedom to select the curriculum and major of my choice?

We have all heard the stories, real or embellished, of athletes majoring in basket weaving. Schools and conferences today pay much closer attention to graduation rates. However, programs are still out there that are interested in keeping the student-athlete eligible above all else, including education. The athletic department should provide guidance on curriculum decisions, but the student-athlete should have the freedom to make the final choice.

16. Under what conditions or circumstances are scholarship athletes cut from the athletic program?

Every student-athlete enters college with high expectations.

Sometimes those lofty goals are not fulfilled. You do not have to make all-American or all-league or even be a starter to benefit from the college athletic experience. But you must have a good understanding of the rules that apply to your eligibility to retain your benefits. Ask the coach under what circumstances your scholarship can be revoked.

17. What is the existing contract status of the head coach?

This may be a somewhat touchy subject, but it is an important one affecting the next four or five years of your life. Sometimes the most frustrated athletes are those who were recruited by one coach but who then must serve another. Try to determine the stability of the current head coach. Take a look at team wins and losses and other factors, and be realistic when evaluating whether a coach is on thin ice or likely to move on to a greener pasture. College coaching is a very unstable and insecure profession and you should take this into account. Don't hesitate to ask the coach what his or her career goals are for the next four years.

18. Does your college have a job placement office? What percentage of graduating seniors find jobs?

In any college selection process, the student should investigate the institution's ability to place its students on the proper career path. Most colleges maintain a job placement office that specializes in introducing students to postgraduate career opportunities. College coaches should be familiar with their university's job placement office and should take a proactive interest in introducing these resources to their student-athletes. Prospects should also inquire about the

existence of graduate assistant programs. Many college athletic programs provide part-time coaching and administrative jobs for deserving student athletes interested in pursuing graduate school. So ask also if graduate assistant programs exist for student-athletes who are interested in graduate school.

19. *Is any part of the athletic program currently under
sanction or probation of any kind for rules violations?*

While this is an important consideration, a school serving
some type of penalty for rules violations does not necessarily deserve to be eliminated from your list; violations could
have occurred under previous coaches or may be attribut-
able to extenuating circumstances. The important issues to
consider are how extensive the penalties are and whether
the school has moved to correct the problems. You should
also be aware of any current investigations underway by
the NCAA, conference, or school.

20. *Finally, ask your recruiter or coach about the ways you
will benefit from the program over the next four years.
Will you be in a better position to face the challenges of
life?*

There is no single right answer to this question, but the tone
and substance of the answer can tell you a lot about the sincerity of the coach and his or her belief in the school and
athletic program the coach represents. Coaches should not
be focusing on your chances of becoming an all-American
or on a career in the pros. Instead, they should be concen-

trating on relating to you as a student-athlete, the academic and social benefits of attending their respective universities.

Five Important Questions To Ask Yourself

1. *Does this institution offer curriculum opportunities in my field of interest?*

Remember that you are selecting not only an athletic program but an institution that will serve as the foundation for molding your career after competitive athletics. Like many students entering college, you may not have yet selected a major or a career, but you will probably have developed some exploratory interests. Make sure the school curriculum provides an opportunity to answer some of your career questions.

2. *Is this institution geographically compatible with my needs and those of my family?*

Sometimes, in the excitement and allure of pursuing college athletics, a student-athlete can overlook a basic need. Consider location as a key element in your analysis. Geographical requirements will vary with the individual; too close may be just as undesirable as too far. Discuss with family members their mobility and ability to travel to your campus, if this is important to you.

3. *Will the institution provide me with a comfortable social environment in terms of size, population, and setting?*

Always remember that you are selecting not only an athletic program and an academic environment but also your home for at least the next four years. It is important to feel comfortable with the school, its setting, and its population. A visit to the school is always an important step. While there, make sure you take the time to discuss life on campus with current students.

4. Do I have a positive impression of the coaching staff at this school?

Of all the guidelines that can be suggested as criteria for selecting an athletic program, the most important should be your feeling for the coaches. You will be directly influenced for the next four years more by the coach than by anyone else on campus. The coach is the one making you an offer, and he or she is the one who can also take it away. Try to get to know the head coach, as well as the assistant coach, well in advance of your final commitment.

5. If my athletic career ended on the first day of class, could I be happy at this school for the next four years?

In the final analysis, the answer to this question summarizes your evaluation. Athletics is a major part of your life, but it is only a single element of your education. Your education will continue after the practices, the games, and the competition. Your education will even continue after graduation. The best choice is a school that lays a strong foundation for your continuing education, with or without sports.

13.   Step-by-Step Guide

The Road to Athletic Scholarship Fifteen Key Points

1. Recognize that you, as a student-athlete, have a committed interest in pursuing a college athletic *and academic* career. Don't just pay lip service to an academic commitment. Internalize the necessity of succeeding in the classroom.

2. Share your desire and commitment to compete at the collegiate level with your parents, high school coach, and guidance counselor. While we are all, at times, reticent to share our dreams, it is important for you, as a student-athlete, to share this goal with your support

group. Unless you are one of the rare "blue chip" prospects, you will need all the help you can get to identify, contact, visit, and interview with college recruiters.

3. Identify junior colleges, colleges, or universities that are compatible with your interests (academic, social, and athletic) and potential level of skill. Create a list. (See the college directory list in the appendix.) This prospect list should be a product of input from your high school coaches, parents, and any feedback you have received from college recruiters. It is always a good idea to have a few schools on your list that you believe to be closely compatible with your abilities. But it is also a good idea to include several schools that you view as beyond your abilities (academically as well as athletically) as well.

4. As early as possible (as a freshman, a sophomore, or, at the latest, a junior), write to the athletic offices of target schools on your list. Introduce yourself (see the sample letter in the Appendix) and request information on your individual sport. At the same time, call or write to each school's admissions office and request information on admissions and curriculum. (See the sample letter in the Appendix.) Also, determine your target schools' affiliation (to the NCAA, NAIA, or NJCAA) and call or write to these associations for the appropriate athletic recruiting handbooks and literature. (See the Appendix.) Familiarize yourself with this information. Play by the rules at all times!

5. Review the institutions' entrance requirements and the proper association (NCAA, NAIA, etc.) guidelines for scholarship eligibility. Review this information with your guidance counselor and/or coach.

6. Contact the target schools' financial aid offices no later than your junior year, to determine what type of financial aid or loans are available to students with your qualifications. Review this information with your parents and guidance counselor.

7. When schools begin to show an interest in you, they may request a film, depending on your particular sport. Ask your coach about the availability of a film. Share the feedback with your parents. If necessary, ask your parents to obtain or create a film and mail it to the college recruiters on your list. This should occur by the end of your junior year, if possible.

8. Personally visit as many schools as possible on your list. If you cannot visit the schools, inquire of friends and relatives who may have knowledge of them. But there is no substitute for the personal visit. You can be surprised how perception is not always reality. This is true of the physical campus as well as of the coaches and professors who represent the institution. Athletically, it is always a plus to observe how the coaches treat current players and how those athletes respond to coaches. You will find that most student-athletes at universities will

be quite candid about how they feel about the school and the coaching staff.

9. Get answers to the twenty-five questions found in chapter 12.

10. If recruiters are not responding in a positive manner to your candidacy, reevaluate your list and create additional alternatives. Do this no later than the beginning of your senior year.

11. If no scholarship offers are forthcoming, give strong consideration to "walking onto" an athletic program and earning a scholarship in later years. When considering walking on, do so only on the encouragement of the recruiting coaches at that school. Realize that the decision to walk on may not lead to scholarship. Discuss with your parents your financial capabilities to stay in school without an athletic grant. More than ever, make certain you could be happy at this school without athletics in the equation. When comparing walk-on options, lean toward the "most likely to fit in" category rather than the "most challenging." By trying to walk on, you have already given yourself a serious challenge. Finally, get a clear understanding from the college coach about the differences in benefits, schedules, and requirements of a scholarship athlete and those of a walk on participant. But all student-athletes must understand that successful walk-ons at scholarship schools are the

exception and not the rule. The larger the school and the more scholarships it offers, the more the odds of successfully walking on decrease significantly. Many Division 1-A and Division II schools rely on walk-ons to fill out their programs, but large Division I schools generally rely on scholarship players—particularly in the highly visible sports such as football, basketball, and baseball.

12. If you have received scholarship offers, confer with your parents, coach, and school counselor to narrow your choices down to the right school for you.

13. The final decision on a school must rest with the individual student-athlete. Factor in the opinions of others, but go to a school that satisfies as many of *your* needs (athletic, academic, and social) as possible.

14. Make sure you have obtained acceptance from the desired college admissions office. (Check with your high school guidance counselor). Make sure, when signing a scholarship of any kind, that it is binding and within the rules set forth by the school and the proper governing body (NCAA, NAIA, etc.). Ask for verification from not just the recruiter but also the head coach of the college that is extending the offer. Require that all conditions of the athletic grant are presented to you *in writing* and are signed by the head coach and/or athletic director.

15. Remember that the successful signing of an athletic scholarship is only the beginning of a new phase of your life. You are accepting a challenge that will require a much higher degree of sacrifice, focus, and determination. Be ready when you get there.

Appendix

Contents for Appendix

College Athletic Associations   123
College Athletic Directories   125
Sample Letters for the Student-Athlete   127
Standard College Athletic Recruiting Forms   131

Collegiate Athletic Associations

Use this listing to obtain handbooks from the appropriate collegiate governing body on the rules and regulations of college athletic recruiting. Remember that member schools of these organizations may also have rules and regulations over and above those enforced by their respective governing body. Contact the association and the individual schools regarding any specific questions on recruiting guidelines. *Always play by the rules*!

  ✍ National Association of Intercollegiate Athletes (NAIA)
1221 Baltimore Avenue
Kansas City, Missouri 64105
Phone: 816-842-5050

Publications
A Guide for the College-Bound Student
A New Definition of Success (Brochure)
NAIA Official Handbook

  ✍ National Collegiate Athletic Association (NCAA)
6201 College Boulevard
Overland Park, Kansas 66211-2422
Phone: 913-339-1906

Publications
NCAA Guide for the College-Bound Student-Athlete (free)
Coaches Recruiting Guide (individual sports)

🖉 National Junior College Athletic Association (NJCAA)
   P.O. Box 7305
   Colorado Springs, Colorado 80933-7305
   Phone: 719-590-9788

   Publications
   Official Handbook and Casebook ($7)

College Athletic Directories

The following publications print listings of colleges around the country. Use these sources to identify target schools for your consideration. Also, consult with your parents, high school coach, and guidance counselor to focus on schools that are most likely to satisfy your individual talents and needs. Your list should be comprised of schools that satisfy your academic, social, and geographic needs as well as your athletic aspirations.

1. *The National Association of Intercollegiate Athletes (NAIA)*

The NAIA publishes a listing of all member schools with the name, and the full address of each. The book is furnished to members of the NAIA for $25 and to the public for $100.

2. *The National Collegiate Athletic Association (NCAA)*

Call or write to the NCAA and request a listing of colleges in your category of athletic interest (basketball, swimming, etc.). The NCAA will mail to you, free of charge, a listing of schools with the city, state, and zip code of each.

3. *The National Junior College Athletic Association (NJCAA)*

Call or write for their *Official Handbook and Casebook*. The book lists all NJCAA schools, broken down by region, with the name of each school and its full address.

4. *The 1995–96 National Directory of College Athletics*

(Printed by Collegiate Directories, Inc., P.O. Box 450640,

Cleveland, OH 44145.) This comprehensive directory lists all colleges and universities nationwide and includes sports categories, names of coaches, and the complete address and phone number for each school. The directory can be obtained by sending $27.95 for the men's edition or $19.95 for the women's edition, plus $2.50 shipping and handling for each order. For additional information call 216-835-1172.

Sample Letters for the Student-Athlete

This section contains sample letters of introduction that will be useful for the student-athlete when communicating with college coaches, admissions offices, and financial aid officers. Use these letters as guidelines and feel free to include other information you deem relevant. (Please note: The addresses on these letters are not complete. Refer to one of the college directories mentioned in the previous section for the correct address and person to contact.)

Sample Student-Athlete Letter to a College Athletic Program

Basketball Office
University of Georgia
Athens, Georgia 00000

Dear Coach:

My name is Brett Smith, and I am a junior at George Walton
High School in Marietta, GA. Currently, I am a starter on the
varsity team at Walton High, at the #2 guard position. I am 6'2"
and weigh 180 pounds. I am very interested in continuing my
basketball career at the University of Georgia.

Please contact my high school coach, Joe Jones, at (404) 100-1000
for more information regarding my high school courses and
college potential. In the interim, I would greatly appreciate the
opportunity to learn more about the University of Georgia basketball program and also the curriculum options at your fine
school.

Thank you for your assistance. I look forward to hearing from
you and hope you will feel free to contact me at the address and
phone number below.

Sincerely,

Brett Smith

Brett Smith
4500 Powers Ferry Road
Atlanta, GA 00000
(404) 100-0000

Sample Student-Athlete Letter to College Admissions Office

Office of Admissions
University of California
Division of Student Affairs
118 Academic Building
Berkley, California 00000

Dear Admissions Officer:

My name is Scott Brown, and I am a junior at Heritage High
School in Sacramento, California. I am very interested in knowing
more about the University of California and the requirements for
admission. Please forward to me information on the curriculum
offered by the University of California and the general guidelines and requirements for admission.

Thank you for your assistance. I eagerly look forward to learning
more about your fine school.

Sincerely,

Scott Brown

Send information to:

Scott Brown
250 Elm Street
Sacramento, California 00000

Sample Student-Athlete Letter to College Financial Aid Office

Office of Financial Aid
Tulane University
New Orleans, LA 00000

Dear Financial Aid Officer:

My name is Sara Thompson, and I am a junior at Allen High
School in Marietta, Georgia. I am interested in attending Tulane
University and would therefore appreciate any information you
might send me regarding financial assistance available to Tulane
students, including scholarships, loans, and work programs.

Thank you for your assistance. I eagerly look forward to learning
more about financial aid opportunities at Tulane University.

Sincerely,

Sara Thompson

Send information to:

Sara Thompson
410 Maple Road
New Orleans, LA 00000

Standard College Athletic Recruiting Forms

This section includes examples of standard recruiting forms sent by college recruiters to high school student-athletes, the high school coach, and the high school administrative office. A study of these forms reveals that most colleges are looking for more than just "athletes." They are seeking well-rounded individuals who will make a positive contribution to the college or university academically and socially as well as athletically.

Sample Academic Form Sent to Student-Athlete's High School

General Academic Questionnaire

1. Name of Student _____

last   _first_

2. Address _____
                       street

city   _state_   _zip_

3. Year in School _____

4. Class Rank: Stood _____ in a class of _____students at the end of the _____ year.
(*If exact rank has not been determined, please indicate the appropriate rank in class.*)

5. Scores on Standard Tests:

    a. Preliminary Scholastic Assesment Test:
       Verbal _____ Math _____
    b. Scholastic Assesment Test:
       Verbal ____ Math _____
       Achievement scores _____
    c. National Merit Scholarship Test:
       Total Composite Score (percentile) _____
    d. I.Q. _____
    e. Other test scores: _____

6. Would you recommend this student as being academically qualified for our university? ☐ Yes ☐ No

7. Remarks: _____

_____

—continued—

8. Name of High School Coach: _____

Date _____

Signed _____

(principal) _____

School _____

Address _____

Zip _____

Telephone _____

Sample Recruiting Form Sent to Student-Athlete—Football

Social Security No.Date _____

Name _____
      last   *first*   *Initial*
Nickname _____

Address _____

City _____ State _____ Zip _____

Home Phone ( ) _____

Date of Birth _____

High School _____

School Phone ( ) _____

School Address _____

City _____ County _____ State _____ Zip _____

Father's Name _____
Occupation _____
College _____

Mother's Name _____
Occupation _____
College _____

Marital Status:
☐ Married ☐ Divorced ☐ Separated ☐ Deceased

Brothers Sisters—Names and Ages _____

_____

Person you know who has attended this university:

Name _____

Relationship _____

—continued—

134

Test Scores   PSAT: V _____ M _____
                    SAT—Jr.: V _____ M _____
                    Sr.   V _____ M _____

ACT: Composite _____

English _____   Math _____

Soc. Studies _____   Nat. Science _____

Grade Point Avg. _____   Rank in Class _____

Total Number in Class _____ Year of Graduation _____

Achievement Scores _____ / _____

Will you apply for financial aid?   ☐ Yes   ☐ No

Your plans for a college major _____

Other schools of interest _____

Sr. Counselor's Name _____

Office Phone (_____) _____

Height _____   Weight _____

Position Played: Offense _____   Defense _____

40 Yd. Time _____ Shorts _____ Pads _____

Bench Pr. _____   Jersey No._____ Light _____

Dark _____   Specialities _____

Other Sports Played _____

H.S. League _____

Honors _____

Coach's Name _____

Home Phone (_____) _____

Sample Recruiting Form Sent to Student-Athlete—Basketball

Name _____
              last   *first*   *middle*

Nickname _____

Home Address _____
                             street

_____
             city   *state*   *zip*

Home Phone (_____) _____

Date of Birth _____ Age _____ Height _____ Weight _____

Position _____

High School _____

Coach's name _____

High School Phone (_____) _____

Coach's Home Phone (_____) _____

High School Address _____
                             street

_____
             city   *state*   *zip*

College requires the SAT or ACT and, at times, three
achievement tests (English Comp., plus two others)

PSAT: V _____ M _____ Date _____

SAT: V _____ M _____ Date _____

ACT: _____ Date _____

Achievement Scores:

English Comp. _____ #2 _____ #3 _____

Class Rank _____ Grade Point Average _____

—continued—

Intended Major: _____

1st Choice _____

2d Choice _____

Please list athletic honors:

_____

_____

Parent or Guardian _____

Occupation _____

Guidance Counselor _____

Date of Graduation _____

Sample Recruiting Form Sent to Student-Athlete—Swimming

• • • PERSONAL INFORMATION • • •

Date _____

Name_____
       last   *first*   *middle*

Nickname _____

Address _____
                            street

_____
       city   *state*   *zip*

Best times to reach you by phone: _____

Phone (____) _____

Age ____ Birthdate ____   Height ____ Weight ____

Date of Graduation ____ Social Security Number _____

Parents Names _____

Family members that attended this college

_____

People you know currently attending this college

_____

• • • SCHOOL AND SWIM CLUB INFORMATION • • •

High School _____ Phone (____)_____

HS Coach's Name _____Phone (____)_____

Swim Club _____

Coach _____ Phone (____)_____

• • • ACADEMICS • • •

Grade Point _____   (on a scale of   )

Class Rank _____   of _____

• • • *Please forward a copy of your transcript to the Swimming Office* • • •

—continued—

PSAT: V _____ M _____ SAT: V _____ M_____
ACT Scores _____ ACT Composite _____

Achievement Test Scores

American History _____   Biology _____
Chemistry   _____   English _____
French   _____   German _____
Latin   _____   Math I _____
Math II   _____   Physics _____
Russian   _____   Spanish _____
Other   _____   Other _____

   • • • *Please keep the Swimming Office updated on your test scores* • • •

Anticipated major (or areas of interest) _____

Are you currently planning on applying? ☐ YES ☐ NO

Do you plan to apply Early Decision? ☐ YES ☐ NO

Other schools applied to _____

Will you be applying for financial aid? ☐ YES ☐ NO

Honorary or need-based? _____

• • • SWIMMING and DIVING PARTICULARS • • •
Please list YARD times

Freestyle

50 ____ 100 ____ 200 ____ 500 ____ 1000 ____ 1650 ____

Backstroke ____ 100 ____ 200 ____

Butterfly ____ 100 ____ 200 ____

Breaststroke ____ 100 ____ 200 ____

Ind. Medley ____ 200 ____ 400 ____

   • • • *Please update the Swimming Office as your best times change* • • •
Number of years swimming competitively _____

Average daily yardage _____

Number of workouts per week _____

Divers: List highest score achieved:1 Meter ____ 3 Meter __

Divers: Please give your 1- and 3-meter lists on an attached form.

OTHER PARTICULARS—Awards, medals, etc., please list on an
attached form.

Sample Recruiting Form Sent to Student-Athlete—Track and Field

Date _____

Full Name _____
           last   *first*   *middle*

Nickname _____

Home Address _____
                      street

_____
city   *state*   *zip*

Phone (___) _____
Date of Birth _____ Age _____ Date of Graduation _____
Height _____ Weight _____

Parent's Full Name _____
Occupation _____

High School _____
Track Coach _____

School Address _____

_____

List your track event(s): Best three performances
(time or distance, meet)

1. _____

2. _____

3. _____

Other sports participated in _____

_____

Honors received _____

_____
                                       —continued—

Name the outstanding trackmen you competed against this year and name of high school they attended:

Name _____

Event/Performance _____

School and Address _____

Name _____

Event/Performance _____

School and Address _____

Name _____

Event/Performance _____

School and Address _____

Check your estimated scholastic rank in class:

☐ Top 10%   ☐ Top 25%   ☐ Top 50%   ☐ Lower 50%

College requires the SAT exam and three achievement tests (English Comp. plus two others)

Scores on standard tests if available:
1. Scholastic Assesment Test (SAT) of College Board:
Verbal _____ Mathematical _____

2. Achievement Scores _____

3. National Merit Scholarship Test: _____
Total Composite Score (percentile)

Have you already applied?   ☐ YES   ☐ NO
Shall we send application forms?   ☐ YES   ☐ NO

What college course are you interested in taking? (Major)

_____

Dear Coach:

In preparation for this year's recruiting, we are attempting to gain a detailed athletic evaluation of all prospects who have been recommended to us. Would you be kind enough to complete the enclosed form and return it to our office?

If you have any other athletes you would like to recommend, do not hesitate to include them on the return form.

Thank you again for your time and consideration. We feel the coach's personal recommendation is very important to our evaluation of high school athletes. This form will be held in the strictest of confidence.

Sincerely,

Assistant Head Coach

University—Football Evaluation Form

Name: _____

Class: _____ Telephone: _____

Address: _____

_____

City_____ State: _____ Zip _____

Ht: _____ Wt: _____ Off Pos: _____ Def: _____

40yd: _____ Bench: _____ Squat _____

What level of football can he play?

(Circle One)   Div.1A   Div. 1AA   Div. II   Div. III

How many years could he play at a 1-AA school?

(Circle One)   1   2   3   4

—continued—

Recommended best position at college: Off _____ Def _____

Rating:

(4) Outstanding   (3) Good   (2) Average   (1) Poor

____Character   ____Skills for position

____Dedication to football   ____Quickness for position

____Does he want to be good?   ____Total athletic ability

____Work habits   ____Size potential

____Coachability   ____Strength

____Competitive   ____Football intelligence

____Plays with pain   ____Hitter/physical player

Honors: #Letters _____   Captain____

                     All-League_____   All-State_____

Other sports (circle):   Basketball

                             Baseball

                             Track

                             Wrestling

                             Others _____

General Comments _____

_____

High School: _____

Head Coach: _____

Sample Recruiting Form Sent to Student-Athlete—Golf Team

Name _____

Address _____

_____

Telephone _____ Date of Birth: _____

High School Graduation Date _____

Parents' Name _____

Parents' Occupation _____

Age _____ Weight _____ Height _____

High School Attended _____

PSAT _____Verbal _____ Math _____

SAT _____Verbal _____ Math _____

ACT _____ _____ _____ _____ _____(cum.)

Class Rank _____ Grade Point Average _____

Possible College Major _____

Students or alumni you know from this school: _____

_____

Home Course _____

Professional _____

Course Rating _____

Handicap _____

Average Score _____

—continued—

My application has been made for the fall of _____
                                              year

Please check one of the following:

_____ I would like Early Decision on my application made on December 15. (Your *final*, not preliminary, application must be received in the Admissions Office by November 8.)

_____ I would like a decision on my application made on April 15. (Your final, not preliminary, application must be received in the Admissions Office by January 15.)

Sample Athletic Prospect Questionnaire—Baseball

Date _____

PERSONAL INFORMATION

Social Security # _____

Last Name _____

First Name _____ M.I. _____

Nickname _____

Mailing Address _____

City _____ State _____ Zip _____

Home Phone No. (_____) _____ Birthdate _____

FAMILY INFORMATION

Parents/Guardians	College Attended	Year	Occupation

Brothers/Sisters	College Attended	Year	Age

Alumni you know	Year	Relative	
		Yes:	No:
		Yes:	No:
		Yes:	No:

Current students you know	Year	Relative	
		Yes:	No:
		Yes:	No:
		Yes:	No:

Will you apply for financial aid?   Yes: _____ No: _____

Parents' marital status (can impact financial aid forms needed)

Married: Separated: Divorced: Remarried: Deceased:

—continued—

ACADEMIC INFORMATION

Year of Graduation _____

High School _____ H.S. Code _____ H.S. City _____ H.S. State

College Counselor _____ Phone (___)

Grade Point Average _____ Rank# _____ in class of _____

Honor Courses _____

Language Courses _____

Math Courses _____

Soc. Stud. _____

Science _____

Possible College Major _____

Have you applied? Yes: _____ No: _____

Other schools to which you will apply _____

Test Scores	PSAT	V		M	
Junior	SAT	V		M	
Senior	SAT	V		M	
Achievement Tests					
ACT Composite	English			Math	

BASEBALL INFORMATION

Position(s) played _____

Bat:Throw _____

Summer Baseball experience _____

Batting Average _____

W–L (Record) _____ E.R.A. _____

Major League Scout Reference _____

_____

_____

Sample Athletic Prospect Questionnaire—Cross-Country (Women)

Date _____

PERSONAL INFORMATION

Social Security # _____

Last Name _____

First Name _____ M.I._____

Nickname _____

Mailing Address _____

City _____ State _____ Zip _____

Home Phone No. (_____) _____ Birthdate _____

FAMILY INFORMATION

Parents/Guardians	College Attended	Year	Occupation

Brothers/Sisters	College Attended	Year	Age

Alumni you know	Year	Relative	
		Yes:	No:
		Yes:	No:
		Yes:	No:

Current students you know	Year	Relative	
		Yes:	No:
		Yes:	No:
		Yes:	No:

Will you apply for financial aid?   Yes: ____ No: ____

Parents' marital status (can impact financial aid forms needed)

Married: Separated: Divorced: Remarried: Deceased:

—continued—

ACADEMIC INFORMATION

Year of Graduation _____

High School	H.S. Code	H.S. City	H.S. State

College Counselor _____ Phone (___) _____

Grade Point Average _____ Rank# _____ in class of _____

Honor Courses _____

Language Courses _____

Math Courses _____

Soc. Stud. _____

Science _____

Possible College Major _____

Have you applied?   Yes: _____ No: _____

Other schools to which you will apply _____

Test Scores	PSAT	V		M
Junior	SAT	V		M
Senior	SAT	V		M
Achievement Tests				
ACT Composite	English			Math

ATHLETIC INFORMATION

Height _____ Weight _____

Coach's Name _____

College the coach attended _____

Phone   (home) _____

Phone   (work) _____

Honors, records, rankings, etc. _____

Sample Athletic Prospect Questionnaire—Field Hockey

Date _____

PERSONAL INFORMATION

Social Security # _____

Last Name _____

First Name _____ M.I._____

Nickname _____

Mailing Address _____

City _____ State _____ Zip _____

Home Phone No. (_____) _____ Birthdate _____

FAMILY INFORMATION

Parents/Guardians	College Attended	Year	Occupation

Brothers/Sisters	College Attended	Year	Age

Alumni you know	Year	Relative	
		Yes:	No:
		Yes:	No:
		Yes:	No:

Current students you know	Year	Relative	
		Yes:	No:
		Yes:	No:
		Yes:	No:

Will you apply for financial aid?   Yes: _____ No: _____

Parents' marital status (can impact financial aid forms needed)

Married: Separated: Divorced: Remarried: Deceased:

—continued—

ACADEMIC INFORMATION

Year of Graduation _____

| High School | H.S. Code | H.S. City | H.S. State |

College Counselor _____ Phone ( )

| Grade Point Average | Rank# | in class of |

Honor Courses _____

Language Courses _____

Math Courses _____

Soc. Stud. _____

Science _____

Possible College Major _____

Have you applied?   Yes: _____ No: _____

Other schools to which you will apply _____

Test Scores	PSAT	V	M
Junior	SAT	V	M
Senior	SAT	V	M
Achievement Tests			
ACT Composite	English		Math

FIELD HOCKEY INFORMATION

Position (please circle)

Midfield   Forward

Goalie   Defense

Other sports played _____

_____

_____

Sample Athletic Prospect Questionnaire—Lacrosse

Date _____

PERSONAL INFORMATION

Social Security # _____

Last Name _____

First Name _____ M.I._____

Nickname _____

Mailing Address _____

City _____ State _____ Zip _____

Home Phone No. (_____) _____Birthdate _____

FAMILY INFORMATION

Parents/Guardians	College Attended	Year	Occupation

Brothers/Sisters	College Attended	Year	Age

Alumni you know	Year	Relative	
		Yes:	No:
		Yes:	No:
		Yes:	No:

Current students you know	Year	Relative	
		Yes:	No:
		Yes:	No:
		Yes:	No:

Will you apply for financial aid?   Yes: _____No: _____

Parents' marital status (can impact financial aid forms needed)

Married: Separated: Divorced: Remarried: Deceased:

—continued—

ACADEMIC INFORMATION

Year of Graduation _____

High School _____ H.S. Code ___ H.S. City ___ H.S. State

College Counselor _____ Phone ( )

Grade Point Average ___ Rank# ___ in class of

Honor Courses _____

Language Courses _____

Math Courses _____

Soc. Stud. _____

Science _____

Possible College Major _____

Have you applied? Yes: _____ No: _____

Other schools to which you will apply _____

Test Scores	PSAT	V	M
Junior	SAT	V	M
Senior	SAT	V	M
Achievement Tests			
ACT Composite	English		Math

LACROSSE INFORMATION

Position (please circle)

Midfield   Attack

Goalie   Defense

Other sports played _____

_____

_____

Sample Athletic Prospect Questionnaire—Soccer

Date _____

PERSONAL INFORMATION

Social Security # _____

Last Name _____

First Name _____ M.I._____

Nickname _____

Mailing Address _____

City _____ State _____ Zip _____

Home Phone No. (_____) _____Birthdate _____

FAMILY INFORMATION

Parents/Guardians	College Attended	Year	Occupation

Brothers/Sisters	College Attended	Year	Age

Alumni you know	Year	Relative	
		Yes:	No:
		Yes:	No:
		Yes:	No:

Current students you know	Year	Relative	
		Yes:	No:
		Yes:	No:
		Yes:	No:

Will you apply for financial aid?   Yes: _____ No: _____

Parents' marital status (can impact financial aid forms needed)

Married: Separated: Divorced: Remarried: Deceased:

—continued—

ACADEMIC INFORMATION

Year of Graduation _____

High School _____ H.S. Code _____ H.S. City _____ H.S. State _____

College Counselor _____ Phone (___) _____

Grade Point Average _____ Rank# _____ in class of _____

Honor Courses _____

Language Courses _____

Math Courses _____

Soc. Stud. _____

Science _____

Possible College Major _____

Have you applied? Yes: _____ No: _____

Other schools to which you will apply _____

Test Scores	PSAT	V	M
Junior	SAT	V	M
Senior	SAT	V	M
Achievement Tests			
ACT Composite	English		Math

SOCCER INFORMATION

Position (please circle)

Midfield   Defender

Forward   Goalkeeper

Other sports played _____

_____

_____

Sample Athletic Prospect Questionnaire—Softball

Date _____

PERSONAL INFORMATION

Social Security # _____

Last Name _____

First Name _____ M.I._____

Nickname _____

Mailing Address _____

City _____ State _____ Zip _____

Home Phone No. (_____) _____ Birthdate _____

FAMILY INFORMATION

Parents/Guardians   College Attended   Year   Occupation
_____
_____
_____

Brothers/Sisters   College Attended   Year   Age
_____
_____
_____

Alumni you know   Year   Relative
_____ Yes: ___ No: ___
_____ Yes: ___ No: ___
_____ Yes: ___ No: ___

Current students you know   Year   Relative
_____ Yes: ___ No: ___
_____ Yes: ___ No: ___
_____ Yes: ___ No: ___

Will you apply for financial aid?   Yes: _____ No: _____

Parents' marital status (can impact financial aid forms needed)

Married: Separated: Divorced: Remarried: Deceased:

—continued—

ACADEMIC INFORMATION

Year of Graduation _____

High School _____ H.S. Code _____ H.S. City _____ H.S. State

College Counselor _____ Phone ( )_____

Grade Point Average _____ Rank# _____ in class of _____

Honor Courses _____

Language Courses _____

Math Courses _____

Soc. Stud. _____

Science _____

Possible College Major _____

Have you applied? Yes: _____ No: _____

Other schools to which you will apply _____

Test Scores	PSAT	V	M
Junior	SAT	V	M
Senior	SAT	V	M
Achievement Tests			
ACT Composite	English		Math

SOFTBALL INFORMATION

Position(s) played _____

Bat: _____ Throw: _____

Summer softball experience _____

Batting Average: _____ W–L (record): _____ E.R.A. _____

Sample Athletic Prospect Questionnaire—Swimming

Date _____

PERSONAL INFORMATION

Social Security # _____

Last Name _____

First Name _____ M.I._____

Nickname _____

Mailing Address _____

City _____ State _____ Zip _____

Home Phone No. (_____) _____Birthdate _____

FAMILY INFORMATION

Parents/Guardians	College Attended	Year	Occupation

Brothers/Sisters	College Attended	Year	Age

Alumni you know	Year	Relative	
		Yes:	No:
		Yes:	No:
		Yes:	No:

Current students you know	Year	Relative	
		Yes:	No:
		Yes:	No:
		Yes:	No:

Will you apply for financial aid?   Yes: _____ No: _____

Parents' marital status (can impact financial aid forms needed)

Married: Separated: Divorced: Remarried: Deceased:

—continued—

158

ACADEMIC INFORMATION

Year of Graduation _____

High School	H.S. Code	H.S. City	H.S. State

College Counselor _____ Phone ( )

Grade Point Average	Rank#	in class of

Honor Courses _____

Language Courses _____

Math Courses _____

Soc. Stud. _____

Science _____

Possible College Major _____

Have you applied? Yes: _____ No: _____

Other schools to which you will apply _____

Test Scores	PSAT	V	M
Junior	SAT	V	M
Senior	SAT	V	M
Achievement Tests			
ACT Composite	English		Math

SWIMMING INFORMATION

List your events _____ Best times or scores _____

Training distance per day _____ Sessions or days per week ____

Strokes and times or dives and scores _____

Training distance per day _____ Sessions per week _____

Other teams you compete for (USS, YMCA, summer, etc.) _____

Coaches of those teams _____

Sample Athletic Prospect Questionnaire—Tennis (Women)

Date _____

PERSONAL INFORMATION

Social Security # _____

Last Name _____

First Name _____ M.I._____

Nickname _____

Mailing Address _____

City _____ State _____ Zip _____

Home Phone No. (_____) _____Birthdate _____

FAMILY INFORMATION

Parents/Guardians	College Attended	Year	Occupation

Brothers/Sisters	College Attended	Year	Age

Alumni you know	Year	Relative	
		Yes:	No:
		Yes:	No:
		Yes:	No:

Current students you know	Year	Relative	
		Yes:	No:
		Yes:	No:
		Yes:	No:

Will you apply for financial aid?   Yes: _____ No: _____

Parents' marital status (can impact financial aid forms needed)

Married: Separated: Divorced: Remarried: Deceased:

—continued—

ACADEMIC INFORMATION

Year of Graduation _____

| High School | | H.S. Code | H.S. City | H.S. State |

College Counselor   Phone ( )

Grade Point Average   Rank#   in class of _____

Honor Courses

Language Courses

Math Courses

Soc. Stud.

Science

Possible College Major

Have you applied?   Yes: _____ No: _____

Other schools to which you will apply

Test Scores	PSAT	V	M
Junior	SAT	V	M
Senior	SAT	V	M

Achievement Tests

ACT Composite   English   Math

ATHLETIC INFORMATION

Height   Weight

Hand used   Right: Left:

Coach's Name

College the coach attended

Phone (home) ( )

Phone (work) ( )

Videotape available? (circle one)   Yes   No

Honors, records, rankings, etc.

Sample Athletic Prospect Questionnaire—Track

Date _____

PERSONAL INFORMATION

Social Security # _____

Last Name _____

First Name _____ M.I._____

Nickname _____

Mailing Address _____

City _____ State _____ Zip _____

Home Phone No. (_____) _____Birthdate _____

FAMILY INFORMATION

Parents/Guardians	College Attended	Year	Occupation

Brothers/Sisters	College Attended	Year	Age

Alumni you know	Year	Relative	
		Yes:	No:
		Yes:	No:
		Yes:	No:

Current students you know	Year	Relative	
		Yes:	No:
		Yes:	No:
		Yes:	No:

Will you apply for financial aid?   Yes: ____ No: ____

Parents' marital status (can impact financial aid forms needed)

Married: Separated: Divorced: Remarried: Deceased:

—continued—

162

ACADEMIC INFORMATION

Year of Graduation _____

| High School | H.S. Code | H.S. City | H.S. State |

College Counselor   Phone (   )

Grade Point Average   Rank#   in class of

Honor Courses

Language Courses

Math Courses

Soc. Stud.

Science

Possible College Major

Have you applied?   Yes: _____ No: _____

Other schools to which you will apply

Test Scores	PSAT	V	M
Junior	SAT	V	M
Senior	SAT	V	M
Achievement Tests			
ACT Composite	English		Math

TRACK INFORMATION

Height   Weight

Coach's Name

Phone   (home)   (   )

Phone   (work)   (   )

List your events

Best Marks

What has been the highlight of your athletic career?

Do you plan to participate in any other sport in college?

(circle one)   Yes   No   If yes, which sport(s)?

Sample Athletic Prospect Questionnaire—Volleyball

Date _____

PERSONAL INFORMATION

Social Security # _____

Last Name _____

First Name _____ M.I._____

Nickname _____

Mailing Address _____

City _____ State _____ Zip _____

Home Phone No. (_____) _____ Birthdate _____

FAMILY INFORMATION

Parents/Guardians	College Attended	Year	Occupation

Brothers/Sisters	College Attended	Year	Age

Alumni you know	Year	Relative	
		Yes:	No:
		Yes:	No:
		Yes:	No:

Current students you know	Year	Relative	
		Yes:	No:
		Yes:	No:
		Yes:	No:

Will you apply for financial aid?   Yes: _____ No: _____

Parents' marital status (can impact financial aid forms needed)

Married: Separated: Divorced: Remarried: Deceased:

—continued—

164

ACADEMIC INFORMATION

Year of Graduation _____

High School _____ H.S. Code _____ H.S. City _____ H.S. State _____

College Counselor _____ Phone ( )

Grade Point Average _____ Rank# _____ in class of _____

Honor Courses _____

Language Courses _____

Math Courses _____

Soc. Stud. _____

Science _____

Possible College Major _____

Have you applied?   Yes: _____ No: _____

Other schools to which you will apply _____

Test Scores	PSAT	V	M
Junior	SAT	V	M
Senior	SAT	V	M
Achievement Tests			
ACT Composite	English		Math

ATHLETIC INFORMATION

Height _____ Weight _____

Hand used _____ Right: _____ Left: _____

Coach's Name _____

College the coach attended _____

Phone   (home)   (   ) _____

Phone   (work)   (   ) _____

Videotape available? (circle one)   Yes   No

Honors, records, rankings, etc. _____

Sample Athletic Prospect Questionnaire—Wrestling

Date _____

PERSONAL INFORMATION

Social Security # _____

Last Name _____

First Name _____ M.I. _____

Nickname _____

Mailing Address _____

City _____ State _____ Zip _____

Home Phone No. (_____) _____ Birthdate _____

FAMILY INFORMATION

Parents/Guardians	College Attended	Year	Occupation

Brothers/Sisters	College Attended	Year	Age

Alumni you know	Year	Relative	
		Yes:	No:
		Yes:	No:
		Yes:	No:

Current students you know	Year	Relative	
		Yes:	No:
		Yes:	No:
		Yes:	No:

Will you apply for financial aid?   Yes: _____ No: _____

Parents' marital status (can impact financial aid forms needed)

Married: Separated: Divorced: Remarried: Deceased:

—continued—

ACADEMIC INFORMATION

Year of Graduation _____

| High School | H.S. Code | H.S. City | H.S. State |

College Counselor   Phone (   )

| Grade Point Average | Rank# | in class of |

Honor Courses

Language Courses

Math Courses

Soc. Stud.

Science

Possible College Major

Have you applied?   Yes: _____ No: _____

Other schools to which you will apply

Test Scores	PSAT	V	M
Junior	SAT	V	M
Senior	SAT	V	M

Achievement Tests

| ACT Composite | English | Math |

WRESTLING INFORMATION

Background

| Jr. Year | Weight | Record |

Tournament record / results (state, district, etc.)

Background

| Soph. Year: | Weight: | Record: |

Tournament record / results (state, district, etc.)

Greco / Freestyle Tournaments / Results:

Index

Amateur, 68
American College Test (ACT), 45, 46, 47, 48, 50
Athlete counseling, 97
Atlanta Falcons, 2, 4

Beeten, Scott (basketball coach), 56
Black Coaches Association (BCA), 49
Blue Chip (type of student-athlete), 6, 10, 17, 67
Bowden, Bobby, 64

Colgate University, 89
College Scholarship Service (for independent evaluation), 38
Collegiate Commissions Association, 62
Contact, 65
Cornell University, 57

Dallas Cowboys, 85
Dooley, Vince (athletic director), 63, 64
Dunlap, Fred, 3

Eby, Cliff, 72

Feeley, Liz, 89
Financial Aid Form (FAF), 33, 38
Financial need, 37
Florida State University, 63, 64
Full grant-in-aid (from NCAA), 36, 40

General Education Development Test (GED), 51
Georgia Tech, 84

Halfacre, Fritz (coach), 15
Hill, John, 71

Jordan, Michael, 12

King, Walt, 3

Lafayette College, 72, 85
Lambert Cup, 4
Lehigh University, 3, 4, 71, 85
Lewis, Reggie, 56
Lockhardt, John, 33

NAPCO Aluminum Company, 34
National Association of
  Intercollegiate Athletics (NAIA), 28,
  38, 40, 44, 50, 51, 84, 100, 116, 117,
  123, 125
National Collegiate Athletic
  Association (NCAA), 5, 27, 28, 32,
  36–40, 43–50, 59, 60, 62, 65–68, 73,
  76, 78, 79, 83, 100, 102, 106, 108, 112,
  116, 117, 123, 125
National Junior College Athletic
  Association (NJCAA), 29, 39, 40, 44,
  51, 116, 124, 125
National Letter of Intent program,
  62, 63, 64
Northeastern University, 55
Notre Dame, 17, 18, 19

Official Visit, 64
Ohio State University, 84
Olympics, 67, 68
Overbrook Regional High School,
  53, 54, 55, 56

Partial qualifiers, standard for eligi-
  bility, 48
Patriot League, 90
Pell Grant, 34, 36
Pennsylvania Higher Education
  Assistance Agency (PHEAA), 34
Pitt, Tyrone, 53–58

Preferred Walk-on, 92
President's Athletic Conference, 35
President's Commission (ruling
  body of NCAA), 45, 49, 50
Proposition 16, 45, 48
Proposition 48, 45, 48

Qualifiers, standard for eligibility, 48

Recruit, 73, 74
Redshirt, 108
Roasch, Bill, 15

Sample letters, 127–30
Sample recruiting forms, 131–68
Scholastic Assessment Test (SAT), 45,
  46, 47, 48, 50
Simon, Corey, 63, 64
Smith, Jen, 87–90, 94
Stafford Loan, federal subsidized, 34,
  39
Szczypinski, Matt, 31–35

Telephone calls, 66
Thorpe, Jim, 67, 68
Trexler, Dick, 15

University of Georgia, 63, 64, 84
University of Michigan, 84
University of Oklahoma, 84
University of Pennsylvania, 56, 57
University of Texas, 84
Unofficial Visit, 64

Walk-on, 21, 81, 87, 89–94, 118, 123
Washington and Jefferson College,
  33–35
Washington Federals, 4
Washington Redskins, 4, 71, 72, 85
Wichita State, 55